The Sinner from Toledo
and Other Stories

The Sinner from Toledo

and Other Stories

by Anton Chekhov

Translated by
Arnold Hinchliffe

Rutherford • Madison • Teaneck
Fairleigh Dickinson University Press

Library of Congress Catalogue Card Number: 70-147269

Associated University Presses, Inc.
Cranbury, New Jersey 08512

ISBN: 0-8386-7890-4

Printed in the United States of America

Contents

The Sinner from Toledo
and Other Stories

Translator's Introduction

Chekhov's Early Tales

"I have written vaudevilles and Stanislavski has put sentimental dramas on the stage."

IT IS A joke that points to a half-truth—and Anton Chekhov meant it so—but it is a half-truth that has been greatly neglected.

For Chekhov is as much a sharp, perceptive, and ironical writer as he is an introspective and melancholy one. He is humorist as well as poet, rarely sentimental and never self-pitying.

Yet few men had more grounds for self-pity. He knew for most of his writing life the nature of the disease that would torment him more and more and kill him before he was forty-five. But when, at twenty-eight, he looked at the story of his own life, he gave it the strongest of themes:

Could you write a story about a young man, the son of a serf, ex-assistant in a little shop, choir boy, high school and university student, brought up to fawn on rank, kiss the hands of priests, accept other people's ideas without question, offer thanks for every morsel of bread, who is often whipped, goes to lessons without galoshes, fights in the streets, tortures animals, loves dining with rich relatives, and is hypocritical before God and man with no excuse except that he is conscious of his own unimportance—could you write a story of how this young man squeezes the slave out of himself, a drop at a time, and how he wakes one morning to feel that the blood flowing in his veins is real blood, not the blood of a slave?

He was strong-willed, luminously intelligent, and very short of time. Knowing and conquering human weakness in himself, he observed it most sharply, with irony and compassion. There is not a play of his or a short story without a searching gleam, comic or sad or both, on human weakness of one kind or another. It is a theme in all the tales of this collection.

Anton Chekhov was trained and practiced as a doctor. "A man of letters," he wrote, "must be as objective as a chemist . . ." and for him there was no conflict between art and science: both were the study of things as they are, of humanity diagnosed and understood. He saw his people as a doctor does: saw through them, too, like a doctor—amused, forbearing, and without illusion. Testing them on the touchstone of his own nature, he could not despise them without despising himself.

His appetite for human experience was voracious, sensitive, and deep,* and his dream life rich, so that there is vitality and flashing humor in his tales, and wonder and nostalgia.

The tales in this collection are a young man's, all written by his thirty-fifth year, most of them in his twenties. Chekhov is concerned to tell a story with clarity and simplicity and, if need be, with harshness. "What I value," he writes at twenty-three, "are plot and effective protest . . . ," and the earliest of these tales, *The Sinner from Toledo*, written when he was twenty-one, has the bitter drama one would think to find in the work of a young Brecht.

But he is a young man of widening experience. Within the fourteen years these tales are written he takes a degree in medicine; works as doctor, in hospital and privately; travels extensively in South Russia and the Ukraine; crosses Siberia by cart, carriage, and boat to the convict settlement on Sakhalin Island in the Far East; makes during six months there a thorough census and medical report; returns by Singapore, India, Ceylon, and the

---

* "My Holy of Holies is the human body, health, mind, talent, inspiration, love and the most absolute freedom . . ."

Suez Canal; travels the following year to Vienna, Venice, Florence, Rome, Naples, Nice, and Paris; organizes a relief center in the famine-stricken province of Novgorod; buys a farm in a village south of Moscow; and fights a cholera epidemic in the district as "Honorary Medical Superintendent."

For all this he has no advantages of wealth: his father is a failed small-shopkeeper, the son of a serf.

Occasionally he is quite ill and nearly all the time he is writing. (Indeed for a while young Anton's stories keep all other seven members of his family in funds and he is then studying to be a doctor.) He will call some of his earlier work "trash," but soon he is praised by important fellow writers, receives the Pushkin Prize at twenty-eight, and becomes deeply aware of his powers.

He writes hurriedly—"Write, write, write till your fingers break. . . . Don't be disturbed by rejections. Write a story at one go . . ."—trained by the need for immediate impact to mold a strong shape about the hard core of a tale.

His experience acquaints him with almost every kind of person and place. What other young short-story writer can draw characters from so wide a range: henpecked garrison-commander, peasant woman brooding on murder, rheumatic piano-tuner, downtrodden casual mistress, seedy medical student, impressionable schoolgirl, romantic double-bass player, suspected witch, callow sailor, poor sledgeman, adulterous wife, toadying civil servant? Or can depict with such assurance so many varied settings: sordid hotel, vaudeville theatre, sledgeman's shelter, toboggan run, ship at sea, monastery, sexton's lodge?

He is remarkably at ease with his people. There is no hint of condescension, the straining to be fair of Tolstoy and Turgenev, finding it hard to forget they are aristocrats. Making no moral judgment, hampered by no class barrier, Chekhov can see people as they are and as they see themselves.

Though he writes with clarity from wide experience, he also writes compulsively, I think, like his Trigorin in *The Seagull*—"I write ceaselessly, as if hurrying post haste, and I can't do otherwise"—his quick thought evoking vividly the feel of life experienced sharply on the very nerve at a given moment. "A real beauty stood before me," he writes in personal recall, "and I understood it at first glance as I understand a flash of lightning." And in *The Steppe* a young boy feels the tingle on his senses of lightning itself: "Someone seemed to strike a match in the sky—a pale, phosphorescent streak gleamed and went out."

Raissa, "the witch," broods at a window in a storm:

Drops like tears ran down the panes, whitened by short-lived snowflakes which, falling on the glass, glanced at Raissa and melted.

Rebrotyesov remembers a dish of sturgeon:

So savoury was his memory of that sturgeon that the garrison-commander sniffed suddenly the smell of fish and chewed unconsciously, not noticing that mud was gathering in his galoshes.

Iona, the sledgeman, is heavy with grief:

Let his heart break and misery flow out, then it would flood the whole world, so it seems; and yet it is not seen. It is lodged in such an unimportant shell, you couldn't find it with a candle in the daylight.

From this vivid sense of life as immediate experience, Chekhov moves deeper. And here the fact that he begins as comic writer and will always consider himself a humorist* is important. He directs his attention to the points of comic stress, where human folly and weakness are. He sees the ironical pattern in the ordinary, the man behind the rank, the dream behind the posture—a henpecked husband in a garrison-commander, a frustrated would-be father in a philanderer, a thwarted, pompous, pagan lover in a hairy double-bass player, wearing only a top hat and carrying his instrument—the comedy, indeed, behind the tragedy.

For in the sad and bitter stories the approach is the same. In *The Women* Matvei Savitch, who has driven a loving woman to

---

* He will call *The Seagull* and *The Cherry Orchard* comedies despite their sadness.

murder and whose tale will make another brood upon it, tells his own story. We see what he chooses to see of the crisis of his life but we know too the intense emotional involvement of his female listeners, learn their bitter and passionate imaginings. Attention is repeatedly directed to the points of stress where thought and action are at variance, word entangled with deed, illusion with reality: hidden longings, posturings, hypocrisy, and self-deceit are illuminated there. This is a sharpening of perception by irony, a method of deep comedy, and it is highly significant that Chekhov thought of Matvei Savitch as a Russian Tartuffe.

This comic perception of the vulnerable often illuminates love. How many of these tales turn out to be stories of lovers or of those who need love, because it is at the point of irony, of human weakness, that the need is! Iona, the old sledgeman, is weighed down by such need and it makes Aniuta sidle furtively about her student like a spaniel afraid of rebuff. Love is the "glamour" the mean sexton casts over his witch-wife, making her seem "whiter, smoother, more impenetrable," and the *Tears the World Does Not See* are those of Rebrotyesov loving the wife who henpecks him. (And who knows? Perhaps in her pecking there is a kind of love: "Give me my dress from the chair, Mahomet!")

Chekhov was reproached in his own day by Mikhailovski and others for "the lack of an attitude and of moral judgement." Yet he is, in fact, a shrewder social observer because of this "lack." Because he lets his words work for themselves, his characters be themselves, unhampered by praise, blame, or comment, our own imaginative sympathies come into play. Seeing, we try to understand. Because he refrains from judgment, Chekhov comes closer to his people, imagines himself into them, and tests them against his own nature; and at the same time he tests society against suffering human experience. How eloquent a plea is *The Women* for the liberation of women in his day, yet there is not a word of shrill demand! "Effective protest" is implicit in the record of experience.

Because Chekhov's comic method has not been fully appreciated—particularly in the West—and because Stanislavski and his later followers overplayed the melancholy, the early stories have been neglected. One aim of this collection is to restore the balance.

On the other hand, we must not overrate. There is light entertainment, much sheer fun, and some rough-hewn drama here, but clearly the greater work is still to be done. It will be wiser, deeper, and more gentle, the occasional crude edges will be subtly smoothed away. But the robust tang of these early tales, their freshness, clarity, and sparkle will never quite come again.

Imagine the writer, then, as you read his stories: a handsome young man of thirty or so, sensitive and deep, at his table very early before the morning noises of the family disturb him, totally absorbed.

He spent many hours yesterday at his favorite pastime, quiet fishing, or wandering at ease, chewing sunflower seeds like a peasant, brooding on memories for use in this tale.

Now the shape is clear to him and he works quickly, totally committed to his mistress, writing, as to medicine, his wife.

Imagine him, then, as his thought cuts deep in memory and dream to bring forth living people, the spontaneous shock and impact of life itself; at his finest he is seeing and recording at the heart of things, where social pressures hurt most and the need for love is.*

---

* The following stories have, to the best of my knowledge, never before been translated into English: *The Swedish Match, Tears the World Does Not See, Ninotchka, A Stage Manager under the Sofa, Love Affair with a Double-Bass, The Sinner from Toledo, At Sea,* and *A Little Crime*. All the translations in the present collection are by Arnold Hinchliffe.

The Editor

14

The Sinner from Toledo

1881

From the Spanish

WHOEVER REVEALS *the present whereabouts of the witch calling herself Maria Spalanza, or delivers her alive or dead to the court, will receive absolution for his sins.*

This proclamation was signed by the Bishop of Barcelona and four judges on one of those far-off days that will forever remain an indelible blemish on the history of Spain and, perhaps, of humanity.

All Barcelona read the proclamation and searches began. Sixty women, who looked like the wanted witch, were locked up; her relatives were put to the torture. . . .

There was the ludicrous but at that time deeply-held belief that witches had power to turn into cats, dogs or other creatures and certainly black ones. It was told that very often a hunter, who cut off the paw of a creature that attacked him and took it as a trophy, found, on opening his bag, a bloodstained hand, which he recognized as that of his own wife. The people of Barcelona killed all the black cats and dogs, but in none of these unnecessary victims did they recognize Maria Spalanza.

Maria Spalanza was the daughter of a big Barcelona trader. Her father was French, her mother Spanish. From her father she inherited Gallic unconcern and the boundless gaiety so attractive in French women, but from her mother, only her Spanish body. Beautiful, always gay, intelligent, devoting her life to cheerful

15

Spanish idleness and arts, until she was twenty she had not shed a tear. . . . She was happy as a child is happy. . . . On the day when she was just twenty, she married Spalanza, a mariner known to all Barcelona, a handsome Spaniard and, it was said, a learned one. She married because she was in love. Her husband swore to her he would kill himself if she were not happy with him. He loved her to distraction.

On the second day of marriage her fate was decided.

Towards evening she was going from her husband's house to her mother and lost her way. Barcelona is large and not all Spanish women can tell you the shortest way from one end of the city to the other. A young monk met her.

"How do you get to St. Mark's Street?" she asked him.

The monk halted and, pensive, began to look at her. The sun had already set. The rising moon cast its cold rays on Maria's lovely face. Not for nothing do poets, who praise women, speak of the moon! By moonlight a woman is a hundred times more beautiful. Maria's lovely black hair, because of her hurried walking, had spilled out over her shoulders and her deeply-heaving breasts. . . . As she held a kerchief to her neck, she bared her arms to the elbows. . . .

"I swear by the blood of Saint Januarius that you are a witch!" said the young monk suddenly without rhyme or reason.

"If you weren't a monk, I'd think you were drunk!" she said.

"You're a witch!"

The monk muttered an incantation of some kind through his teeth.

"Where's the dog that just ran in front of me? That dog turned into you! I saw it! . . . I know. . . . I've not yet lived to twenty-five but I've caught fifty witches already. You are the fifty-first! I—am Augustin!"

The young monk finished speaking, crossed himself, turned back and went out of sight.

Maria knew Augustin. . . . She had heard a great deal about him from her parents. . . . She knew him as a zealous hunter of witches and as the author of a learned work. In this he cursed women and despised man because he is born of woman.

16

When she had gone half a mile further, she encountered Augustin again. From the gate of a big house with a long Latin inscription four dark figures emerged. They let her go past them and followed her. And in one of them she recognized Augustin. They went with her to her very door.

Three days after the encounter with Augustin a man in black with a swollen, clean-shaven face came to see Spalanza—to all appearances a judge. He ordered him to go at once to the Bishop.

"Your wife is a witch!" the Bishop declared.

Spalanza went pale.

"Give thanks to God!" went on the Bishop. "A man who has from God the precious gift of bringing to the light an evil spirit in a person, opened his eyes for us and you. They saw how she turned into a black dog and how the black dog turned into your wife. . . ."

"She's not a witch but . . . my wife!" muttered Spalanza, stunned.

"She cannot be the wife of a Catholic! She is the wife of Satan! Have you really not noticed, wretched man, that more than once she has already betrayed you for an evil spirit? Go home and bring her here at once. . . ."

The Bishop was a very learned man. He traced the origin of *femina* to two words, *fe* and *minus,* according to the supposedly basic law that a woman has less faith. . . .

Spalanza became paler than a corpse. He left the Bishop's room and clutched his head. Where and to whom could he say that Maria was not a witch? Who would not believe what the monks believed? Now all Barcelona was certain that she was a witch! All! Nothing is easier than to convince a stupid man of a fantastic thing, and all Spaniards were stupid!

"No people are more stupid than the Spanish!" his dying father told him once, and he was a doctor. "Hold Spaniards in contempt and do not believe what they believe!"

Spalanza believed what Spaniards believed but he did not believe the words of the Bishop. He knew his wife very well and was convinced that women only became witches towards old age. . . .

"The monks want to burn you, Maria!" he told his wife as he came home from the Bishop's. "They say that you're a witch and ordered me to take you *over there*. . . . Listen, wife! If you are, in fact, a witch, then God be with you! . . . Turn yourself into a black cat and run away somewhere; but if no evil spirit is in you, I won't hand you over to the monks. . . . They'll put a collar on you and will not let you sleep until you tell lies about yourself. Run away, then, if you are a witch!"

Maria did not turn into a black cat and run away. She only burst into tears and began to pray to God. . . .

"Listen!" Spalanza told his weeping wife. "My late father told me that soon there will come a time when they will laugh at those who believe in the existence of witches. My father was an unbeliever but all the same he told the truth. So you must hide somewhere and wait for that time. . . . It's very easy! The ship of my brother Christopher is being repaired in the harbour. I will hide you on that ship and you will not leave it until that time comes of which my father spoke. . . . According to him that time will come soon. . . .

In the evening Maria lay already deep in the hold of the ship, trembling with cold and fear, as she listened to the noise of the waves and waited impatiently for that impossible time of which Spalanza's father spoke. . . .

"Where is your wife?" the Bishop asked Spalanza.

"She turned into a black cat and ran away from me," he lied.

"I expected and foresaw that! But never mind! We will find her. . . . Augustin has a great gift! Oh, a wonderful gift! Go in peace and next time don't marry a witch! There have been cases when evil spirits passed from wives to husbands. . . . Last year I burned a pious Catholic who, by attachment to an unclean woman, gave up, against his will, his soul to Satan. . . . Be gone!"

Maria lay a long time on the ship. Spalanza visited her every night and brought her all she needed. She lay there a month, another; she lay there a third month but the longed-for time did not come. Spalanza's father was right but months are little to the prejudiced. They cling to life like fish and need whole centuries. . . . Maria became accustomed to her new way of life and even began to laugh at the monks whom she called crows. . . . She would have stayed there longer, sailed away, perhaps, in the repaired ship, as Christopher said, to far countries, very far from stupid Spain, but for a terrible and irreparable mischance.

The Bishop's proclamation, passed around by the people of Barcelona and posted up in all the squares and market places, came into Spalanza's hands. He read it and began to think. The absolution for sins, promised at the end of it, held his attention.

"It would be wonderful to receive absolution!" he sighed.

Spalanza counted himself a terrible sinner. There weighed on his conscience a mass of those sins for which many Catholics went to the stake or died under torture. In his youth he had lived in Toledo, at that time a rallying place of sorcerers and magicians. . . . There, in the twelfth and thirteenth centuries, mathematics flourished more than anywhere else in Europe. From mathematics to magic was in Spanish cities but a single step. . . . Under his father's guidance Spalanza, too, had dealt in magic. He cut open the entrails of animals and gathered strange herbs. Once he crushed something in an iron mortar and there came from it with fearful crash a devil in an outline of blue flame. Life in Toledo was compact of sins like that.

Leaving Toledo after his father's death, Spalanza soon felt terrible pangs of conscience. An old and very learned monk and doctor told him that his sins would never go from him till he received an absolution by some splendid deed. For absolution Spalanza was ready to give up everything if only it would free his soul from the memory of his shameful life in Toledo and keep him from hell fire. He would have given up half his fortune if indulgences had been sold in Spain at that time. . . . He would have gone on foot to holy places, if his business affairs had not prevented him.

"If I weren't her husband, I'd hand her over . . ." he thought, as he read the Bishop's proclamation.

The idea that only a word was needed to get absolution stuck in his mind and gave him no peace by day or night. . . . He loved his wife, he loved her deeply. . . . But for that love, that weakness so despised by monks and even doctors of Toledo, then, very probably, it would have been possible. . . . He showed the proclamation to his brother Christopher. . . .

"I would hand her over," said his brother, "if she were a witch and not so beautiful. . . . Absolution is a splendid thing. . . . But we will not lose it if we wait until Maria's death and hand over her dead body to those crows. . . . Let them burn her dead body. . . . The dead feel no pain. She will die when we are old and in old age we shall need absolution. . . ."

As he said this, Christopher laughed and struck his brother on the shoulder.

"I may die before her," remarked Spalanza. "But I swear by God I'd hand her over, if I weren't her husband!"

A week after this conversation Spalanza paced about the deck and muttered:

"Oh, if she were dead! I won't hand her over alive, no! But I'd hand her over dead! I'd trick those cursed old crows and get absolution from them!"

And Spalanza, in his stupidity, poisoned his poor wife.

Maria's dead body was carried by Spalanza to the court and committed to the flames.

Spalanza received absolution for his sins in Toledo. . . . They forgave him for studying to heal the sick and engaging in the science later to be known as chemistry. The Bishop praised him and gave him a book he had written himself. In it he stated that devils lodge most of all in black-haired women, for black hair has the colour of devils.

At Sea
1883
A Sailor's Story

ONLY VISIBLE were fading lights of the harbour we were leaving and a sky black as ink. A cold, damp wind was blowing. We sensed heavy clouds above us, sensed their will to burst in rain and we were stifled despite the wind and cold.

Crowded in our quarters, we sailors were drawing lots. Our loud drunken laughter burst out, jokes were cracked, someone for fun crowed like a cock.

A little shiver ran over me from head to heel as if at the back of my head were a gap from which a thin, cold shot poured down my naked body. I trembled both for cold and for a reason which I want to tell you now.

Man, in my opinion, is mostly bad, but a sailor, I admit, is sometimes worst of all on earth, worse even than foul beasts who after all have the excuse of giving in to instinct. It may be I am wrong, for I don't know life but all the same it seems to me a sailor has more cause to hate and curse himself than anyone else at all. A man who at any moment could fall from the mast and disappear forever under the waves, who only knows God when he's drowning or dying, such a man needs nothing and pities nothing on the land. We drink a lot of vodka, we debauch ourselves, for we see no use to anyone or anything in a virtuous life at sea.

However, I'll continue.

We were drawing lots. Apart from those on watch or busy

there were twenty-two of us. To just two of that number would fall the chance of enjoying a rare sight. The fact was that the "bridal cabin" on our ship had passengers that night and in its walls were just two holes, which we could use. One hole I cut myself with a thin file after piercing the wall with a corkscrew, the other a fellow sailor had carved out with his knife. We had both worked more than a week.

"One hole is for you!"

"For who?"

They pointed at me.

"Whose is the other?"

"Your father's!"

My father, an old bent seaman with a face like a baked apple, came up to me and tapped my shoulder.

"Today, my lad, we're lucky together," he said to me. "Do you hear, my lad? Luck's come to you and me at the same time. It means something, that does."

Impatiently he asked the time. It was only eleven.

I went out of our quarters, smoked my pipe and began to look at the sea. It was dark but I daresay my eyes reflected what went on in my mind as I made out shapes against the dark background of night and saw what I so lacked in my still young but already misspent life. . . .

At twelve I went past the passengers' lounge and peeped through the door. The bridegroom, a young parson, fair-haired and good-looking, was sitting at a table with a prayer book in his hands. He was explaining something to a tall, thin English-woman. The bride, young, slender and very pretty, sat beside her husband, her blue eyes never leaving his blond face. A tall, plump Englishman was walking up and down the room, an old banker with an ugly red face. He was the husband of the elderly lady to whom the bridegroom was talking.

"Parsons usually talk for hours at a time!" I thought. "He won't stop till morning!"

At one o'clock my father came to me and pulled me by the arm.

"It's time!" he said. "They've come out of the lounge."

22

In a flash I rushed down a steep stairway and turned to the familiar wall. Between it and the ship's side was a place full of soot, water and rats. Soon I heard the heavy steps of my old father. He stumbled against bags and tins of kerosine and cursed.

I felt for my hole and pulled out the square-shaped piece of wood I'd taken so long to cut. And I saw a thin, transparent muslin through which there came to me a soft, pink light, and with the light there wafted to my burning face a stifling and supremely pleasant scent: that, most probably, of the aristocratic boudoir. To see the boudoir I had to push aside the muslin with two fingers, which I hastened to do.

I saw bronze, velvet, lace. And all was bathed in pink light. Three yards from my face was a bed.

"Let me come to your hole," said my father, poking me impatiently in the side. "The view's better in yours."

I was silent.

"Your eyes are stronger than mine, lad. Surely it's all the same to you if you look from far or near!"

"Hush!" I said. "Don't make a noise, they'll hear us!"

The bride sat on the edge of the bed, dangling her little feet on fur. She was looking at the ground. Her husband, the young parson, stood before her. He was saying something to her but what it actually was—I don't know. The noise of the ship prevented me hearing. The parson was speaking hotly, making gestures, eyes glittering. She listened and shook her head.

"Hell! A rat bit me!" muttered my father.

I pressed my chest tighter against the wall as if I feared my heart would burst out. My head was burning.

The couple went on talking for a long time. Then the parson got down on his knees, stretched out his arms towards her and began to plead. She shook her head. He stood up at that and walked to and fro. From his expression and the way he moved his hands I guessed that he was making threats.

His young wife rose to her feet, walked slowly towards the wall where I was standing and stopped just by my hole. She stood motionless, preoccupied, and I devoured her face with my eyes. I felt she was suffering, fighting with herself, floundering,

23

and at the same time her features showed anger. I understood nothing.

For five minutes probably we stood face to face like that, then she moved away, stopped in the middle of the cabin and nodded to her parson—in agreement, it seemed. He smiled with pleasure, kissed her hand and went out of the room.

Three minutes later the door opened and the parson came in, behind him the tall, plump Englishman I mentioned earlier. The Englishman went up to the bed and asked the pretty girl a question of some sort. Pale, not looking at him, she nodded.

The English banker pulled a kind of bundle from his pocket, a bundle of banknotes probably, and gave it to the parson. He examined and counted them and with a bow went out. The old Englishman locked the door behind him. . . .

I tore myself from the wall as if I'd been stung. I was scared. I felt as if a gale was beating our ship to pieces and we were going to the bottom.

My father, a drunken, debauched old man, took me by the arm and said:

"Let's get away from here! You must not see it! You're only a lad. . . ."

He could scarcely stay on his feet. I carried him up the steep, twisting stairway where real autumn rain was already falling. . . .

The Swedish Match

1883

(A Detective Story)

O N THE MORNING of the 6th of October, 1885, a neatly
   dressed young man came to the office of the Superintendent of Police, 2nd Division, District of S————, and stated
that his master, Mark Ivanovitch Klyauzov, retired guards officer,
had been murdered. He was pale and extremely agitated as he
did so. His hands trembled and his eyes were full of horror.

"Whom have I the honour of addressing?" asked the Superintendent.

"Psiekov, the steward of Klyauzov, agriculturist and me-
chanic."

When the Superintendent reached the scene of the crime,
along with Psiekov and other witnesses, he found this situation.
A crowd was milling about the lodge where Klyauzov lived, for
news of the affair had spread at lightning speed and, because it
was a holiday, they had come flocking from all the nearby vil-
lages. Everywhere were noises and voices, pale, tear-stained faces
glimpsed here and there.

The door to Klyauzov's bedroom was found to be locked.
The key was inside.

"Obviously the villains got in at him through the window,"
remarked Psiekov as they examined the door.

They went into the garden, which the bedroom window over-
looked. The window seemed dark, sinister: it was covered by a

curtain, green and faded, one corner slightly turned up, making it possible to peep into the bedroom.

"Did any of you look in at the window?" asked the Superintendent.

"No, not at all, your honour!" said Ephraim, the gardener, an old man little and grey-haired, looking like a retired N.C.O.

"Ah, Mark Ivanovitch, Mark Ivanovitch!" sighed the Superintendent, gazing at the window. "I told you you'd come to a bad end! I told you, poor fellow— but you wouldn't listen! No good comes of debauchery!"

"We have to thank Ephraim," said Psiekov. "But for him we would never have suspected. He was the first one it occurred to there was something wrong. This morning he came to me and said: "Why's the master taking so long to wake up? All week he hasn't been out of the bedroom!" When he told me, I was thunderstruck. . . . The thought came like a flash. . . . He hasn't shown up since last Saturday week and it's Sunday today! Seven days: it's no joke!"

"Yes, the poor devil!" The Superintendent sighed again. "A clever chap, educated, a good sort. In company, you might say, the leading light. But a lecher, heaven help him! I expected this lot!"

"Stepan," he said to one of those who came with him, "off you go this minute to my place and send Andrushka to the Chief Constable with a report. Tell him Mark Ivanovitch has been killed! Yes, and then run for the local Sergeant. Why should he sit easy back there? Let's have him over! And then go quick as you can to Nikolai Yermolaitch, the examining magistrate, and tell him to come here. Wait, I'll write you a note."

The Superintendent set men to watch the lodge, wrote the note and went off to the steward's quarters for a drink of tea. Ten minutes later he sat cautiously crunching sugar and gulping the tea piping hot.

"There you are!" he said to Psiekov. "There you are! A gentleman, a rich man. . . . Favoured by the gods, you might say, as Pushkin puts it, and what comes of all that? Not a thing! He drinks, he seduces . . . and there you are: he gets killed!"

26

Two hours later the examining magistrate arrived. Nikolai Yermolaitch Chubikov, as he was called, was an old man of sixty, big and broad, and occupied in that line for a quarter of a century. He was well known in the district as an honest man, shrewd and active and devoted to his work.

His constant companion, Dukovski, assistant and secretary, came with him to the scene of the crime, a tall young man of twenty six.

"Can this be true, gentlemen?" said Chubikov, coming into Psiekov's room and hastily shaking everyone by the hand. "Can it really? Mark Ivanovitch? Killed? No, it's impossible. Im—poss—i—ble!"

"Well, there you are . . ." sighed the Superintendent.

"Oh, my God! Why, I only saw him last Friday at Tarabankov Fair. I drank, excuse me, gentlemen, some vodka with him!"

"Well, there you are . . ." sighed the Superintendent again.

They murmured, expressed horror, drank a glass of tea and went to the lodge.

"Out of the way!" shouted a constable to the crowd.

Reaching the lodge, the examining magistrate examined first of all the bedroom door. It appeared to be of deal, painted yellow and undamaged. No special marks, likely to yield evidence, were found. They proceeded to break in.

"I beg you, gentlemen, if you've no business here, move off," said Chubikov, as the door, after long smiting and cracking, gave way to the axe and chisel. "In the interests of the investigation, I beg you. . . . Sergeant, let no one in!"

Chubikov, his assistant and the Superintendent opened the door and hesitantly, one after the other, went into the bedroom. This was the sight that met their eyes. In front of the only window stood a big wooden bed with a huge feather mattress. On the rumpled mattress was a hunched-up, rumpled quilt. A pillow in cotton pillow case, rumpled as well, lay on the floor. On a little table by the bed were a silver watch and twenty copeks worth of silver coins; sulphur matches were there too. Except for the bed, the little table and a single chair there was no other furniture.

The Superintendent looked under the bed and saw two dozen empty bottles, an old straw hat and a quart jar of vodka. Under the chair was a single boot covered with dust.

The examining magistrate looked round the room, frowned and went red in the face.

"Villains!" he muttered, clenching his fists.

"But where's Mark Ivanovitch, then?" asked Dukovski, his assistant, quietly.

"I'd rather you didn't interfere!" said Chubikov gruffly. "Please examine the floor . . . Yergraf Kuzmitch," he said, lowering his voice to the Superintendent, "it's the second case of this sort in my experience. In 1870 I'd one just like it. Yes, you must remember. . . . The murder of Portrietov, the merchant. Just the same. The villains killed him and dragged the corpse out through the window. . . ."

Chubikov went to the window, pulled aside the curtain and carefully pushed. The window opened.

"It opens, so it wasn't locked. . . . H'm! Marks on the window-sill, see? Marks made by knees. . . . Somebody climbed out. . . . This window must be thoroughly examined."

"Nothing on the floor of special note," said Dukovski. "No stains, no scratches. I found just one Swedish match, a used one. There it is! As far as I remember, Mark Ivanovitch didn't smoke. For other purposes he used sulphur matches, never Swedish ones. This match may be a clue. . . ."

"Oh . . . be quiet, please!" The examining magistrate flapped his hand. "Keeping on about his match! I can't stand these excitable chaps! Instead of looking for matches you'd better examine the bed!"

Dukovski examined the bed and reported:

"No stains of blood nor any other sort. . . . No recent tears. . . . Marks of teeth on the pillow. . . . Some liquid spilt on the sheet which looks like beer and tastes like it. . . . The bed's general appearance gives reason to think a struggle took place on it."

"I know without you there was a struggle! You're not being asked about a struggle! Instead of looking for struggles you'd better . . ."

28

"One boot is here. The other is not to be seen."

"Well, what about it?"

"Why, it means they smothered him when he was taking his boots off. He hadn't time to take the other off, so . . ."

"He's at it again! . . . And how do you know they smothered him?"

"The marks of teeth on the pillow. And the pillow itself is terribly rumpled and was flung two yards from the bed."

"Doesn't he argue, the blatherer! We'd better go into the garden. You'd better examine the garden instead of rummaging about here. . . . I can do that without you!"

Once in the garden they first examined the grass. Under the window it had been trampled down. And the burdock bush under the window, just against the wall, seemed trampled too. Dukovski was able to find a few broken sprigs of it and a little bit of wadding. On the highest burrs were thin threads of dark blue wool.

"What colour was the suit he wore last?" Dukovski asked Psiekov.

"Yellow. A canvas suit."

"Splendid! So they were wearing dark blue, then."

Some prickly burrs from the burdock were cut off and wrapped carefully in an envelope. At that moment Artsibashev-Svistakovski, the Chief Constable, and Tutuiev, the doctor, arrived. The Chief Constable greeted the others and at once began to satisfy his curiosity; but the doctor, tall and extremely skinny, with sunken eyes, greeted no one, asked no questions, sat down on a stump, sighed and said:

"The Serbians are worked up again! Can't understand what they're after! Ah, Austria, Austria, you're the one behind it!"

Examination of the window from outside yielded absolutely nothing but examination of the grass and bushes round it gave a lot of valuable clues. Dukovski, for example, was able to trace on the grass a long dark streak which stretched from the window many yards into the garden. It ended under one of the lilac bushes in a big, dark-brown stain; and under this very bush they found a boot which seemed the mate of that in the bedroom.

29

"This is blood, shed some time ago!" said Dukovski, examining the stain.

At the word "blood" the ·doctor got up and gave a lazy, cursory glance at the stain.

"Yes, blood," he murmured.

"So he wasn't smothered, if there's blood!" said Chubikov with a spiteful glance at Dukovski.

"They smothered him in the bedroom, then here, fearing he'd come round, they stabbed him with something sharp. The stain under the bush shows he lay there rather a long time while they tried to find some way to carry him from the garden or something to carry him on."

"Well, and what about the boot?"

"That boot confirms me in my opinion that they killed him when he was taking off his boots to go to bed. He took one off, but the other, that's this one, he only managed to get half off. As they dragged him this half-off boot came off by itself."

"Such sharpness, fancy!" chuckled Chubikov. "All cut and dried, all cut and dried! When will you stop your theorizing! Instead of theorizing you'd better take a bit of grass and blood for analysis."

After examining the place and making a plan, the investigators made their way to the steward's quarters to write a report and have lunch. Over lunch they talked.

"Watch, money and the rest . . . all are left untouched," began Chubikov. "As sure as two and two make four, it's clearly a murder without mercenary motive."

"Clearly a murder by a man of standing," said Dukovski.

"What makes you think that?"

"By the evidence of the Swedish match, the use of which is not known yet to peasants here. Only landowners use those matches and not all of them. And, by the way, he was not killed by one man but by three at least. Two held him and the third smothered him. Klyauzov was strong and the murderers must have known it."

"But what use would his strength be to him if he was asleep, say?"

"The murderers came on him as he was taking off his boots. He was taking off his boots, so he couldn't be asleep."

"Theorizing's a waste of time! You'd better eat!"

"It's my belief, your honour . . ." said Ephraim, the gardener, setting up the samovar, ". . . that no one else but Nikolashka did this filthy thing."

"Highly probable . . ." said Psiekov.

"And who is this Nikolashka?"

"The master's personal servant, your honour," replied Ephraim. "Who else could it be, if not him? A ruffian, your honour! A drunk and a woman-chaser, may the Queen of Heaven never permit the like! He was always bringing the master vodka, he used to put him to bed. . . . Who else, then, if not him? And what's more, I'll take the liberty of letting you know, your honour, he boasted, the villain, in the tavern that he'd kill the master. It was all over Akulka, all over a woman. . . . He had a soldier's woman. . . . The master fancied her and took her for himself and he . . . of course . . . got mad. . . . He's slobbering about in the kitchen now, pretending he's sorry about the master . . ."

"And really," said Psiekov, "you can get mad about Akulka. She's a soldier's wife, a peasant girl but . . . Mark Ivanovitch didn't call her Nana for nothing. . . . Something about her makes you think of Nana. . . . She's fascinating. . . ."

"I've seen her . . . I know . . ." said the examining magistrate, blowing his nose in a red handkerchief.

Dukovski blushed and lowered his eyes. The Superintendent drummed with his fingers on a saucer. The Chief Constable coughed and fumbled for something in his briefcase. Only on the doctor, it seemed, the thought of Akulka and Nana made no impression.

The examining magistrate ordered Nikolashka to be fetched. A lanky lad with long, pock-marked nose and hollow chest, in a cast-off coat of his master's, he came into Psiekov's room and bowed down low before the examining magistrate. His face was sleepy and tear-stained and he was quite drunk, could scarcely stand.

31

"Where's your master?" Chubikov asked him.

"He's been killed, your honour."

As he spoke, Nikolashka blinked his eyes and started to cry.

"We know he's been killed. But where's he now? His body, that is, where is it?"

"They say they dragged it through the window and buried it in the garden."

"H'm! . . . They know the results of our inquiry in the kitchen already. . . . That's bad! Well, my good man, where were you on the night your master was killed? On the Saturday, that is?"

Nikolashka lifted his head, craned his neck and pondered.

"I can't think, your honour," he said. "I was drunk and can't remember."

"Alibi!" whispered Dukovski, grinning and rubbing his hands.

"Just so! Well, and why is there blood under your master's window?"

Nikolashka thrust back his head and pondered.

"Be quick and think!" said the Chief Constable.

"Now I know. That blood's from just a little thing, your honour. I cut a hen's throat. I just cut it as usual, but she went and fluttered out of my hands and went running off. . . . That's where the blood came from."

Ephraim confirmed that Nikolashka actually did cut a hen's throat every evening and in different places, but no one saw a half-killed hen running in the garden, though, of course, it was impossible to disprove altogether.

"Alibi!" chuckled Dukovski. "And what a stupid alibi at that!"

"Were you intimate with Akulka?"

"Yes, I sinned."

"And your master took her from you?"

"No, not at all! This is the one who took Akulka from me, Mr. Psiekov here, Ivan Mikhailitch, and it's from Ivan Mikhailitch that the master took her. That's how it was!"

Psiekov was embarrassed and began to rub his left eye. Dukovski scrutinized him, noted the embarrassment and quivered. He saw blue trousers, not previously noticed, on the steward's legs. They reminded him of the blue threads he found on the

32

burdock. Chubikov, in his turn, stared suspiciously at Psiekov.

"Be off!" he said to Nikolashka. "And now please answer one question, Mr. Psiekov. You were here, weren't you, on Saturday last week?"

"Yes, I had supper with Mark Ivanovitch at ten o'clock."

"And then?"

Psiekov was confused and got up from the table.

"Then. . . . Then. . . . I really don't know," he muttered. "I'd drunk a lot at the time. . . . I don't remember where and when I went to sleep. . . . Why are you all looking at me like that? As if I'd killed him!"

"Where did you wake up?"

"I woke up in the servant's kitchen on the stove. . . . Everybody can confirm that. . . . How I came on the stove I don't know. . . ."

"Don't get excited! . . . You consorted with Akulka?"

"No, not particularly . . ."

"Did she move over from you to Klyauzov?"

"Yes. . . . Ephraim, bring some more mushrooms! Would you like some tea, Yergraf Kuzmitch?"

There came a heavy, painful silence and it lasted five minutes. Dukovski remained still, not taking his piercing eyes from Psiekov's paling face. It was the examining magistrate who broke the silence.

"We shall have to go to the big house," he said, "and speak to the dead man's sister, Maria Ivanovna. She may well give us some evidence."

Chubikov and his assistant thanked Psiekov for the lunch and went to the big house. They found Maria Ivanovna, Klyauzov's sister, praying at the high family icons. As she saw the briefcases and the Police caps with badges, she went pale.

"I must first of all ask your pardon for intruding, as it were, on your devotions . . ." began Chubikov with a polite shuffle of the feet. "We've come to you with a request. You've already heard, of course. . . . There's a suspicion that your brother, in some way or other, has been murdered. It's the will of God, you realise. . . . Death spares none, not Czar nor ploughman. Could

33

you help us with evidence of any sort, anything to throw light . . . ?"

"Oh, do not ask me!" said Maria Ivanovna, paler still and hiding her face in her hands. "I can tell you nothing! Nothing! I implore you! There's nothing I . . . What can I say? Oh no, no. . . . Not a word about my brother! I'd die before I tell!"

Maria Ivanovna burst into tears and went into the next room. The investigators looked at one another, shrugged their shoulders and left.

"What a devil of a woman!" cursed Dukovski, as they came out. "Obviously she knows something and is hiding it. And that maidservant's face is covering something . . . Just wait, you devils! We'll have it out, all of it!"

In the evening Chubikov and his assistant travelled home in pale moonlight: sitting in their carriage, both weary and quiet, they sorted out in their minds the events of the day. Chubikov wasn't fond of talking as a rule and Dukovski, who was, stayed silent in deference to the older man. But at the end of the journey he couldn't stand the quiet any longer and began to speak.

"Nikolashka's mixed up in this business," he said. "*Non dubitandum est!* It's plain on his ugly face the sort he is. . . . His alibi gives him away hand and foot. But he's not the instigator, no doubt of that. He was a stupid tool, paid to do it. Do you agree? But that humble Psiekov didn't play a minor role in this. Blue trousers, embarrassment, lying scared on the stove after the murder, that alibi and Akulka."

"Go on, stir away! It's your day, this! According to you, if a man's had Akulka, he's the murderer. Oh, you hothead, you! Should be sucking your dummy, not investigating crimes! You've been after Akulka too: does that mean you're involved?"

"And Akulka lived with you for a month as a cook . . . but . . . I'll say nothing of that. I was playing cards with you the Saturday of the crime, I saw you or otherwise I'd be on your track. The woman's not at the root of this. At the root is the sordid, mean and vicious feeling. . . . That humble young man, you see, didn't fancy being done down. . . . Pride, you see. . . . He longed

34

for revenge. . . . And then! . . . His plump lips show the power of his sensuality. Remember how he licked his lips when he compared Akulka with Nana? No doubt about it: he's burning with passion, the scoundrel! So then: hurt pride and frustrated passion. Enough there to lead to murder. We've got two of them; but who's the third? Nikolashka and Psiekov held him down; but who smothered him? Psiekov is timid, embarrassed, an utter coward. Nikolashka isn't the type to smother with a pillow: he'd use an axe or a blunt instrument. Another, the third one, smothered him. But who?"

Dukovski pulled his cap over his eyes and pondered, saying no word, until the carriage reached the magistrate's house.

"Eureka!" he shouted, going in and taking off his coat. "Eureka, Nikolai Yermolaitch! I don't know why I didn't think of it earlier. Do you know who the third one is?"

"Stop it, please! Look, supper's ready. Sit down and eat it!"

The examining magistrate and Dukovski sat down and had supper. Dukovski poured himself a glass of vodka, rose, and said, eyes shining:

"Do you know who the third one was, then, in league with that villain Psiekov and doing the smothering? It was a woman! Oh yes! I mean the dead man's sister, Maria Ivanovna!"

Chubikov choked over his vodka and stared at Dukovski.

"Are you . . . all right? Your head . . . all right is it? Not aching?"

"I'm perfectly well. But all right, then, let's say I have gone mad. In that case, how do you explain her embarrassment when we arrived? How do you explain her refusal to make a statement? Let's say that's unimportant. Very well! All right! But remember their attitude to one another. She loathed her brother. She's strictly religious. He was a lecher, an atheist. . . . That's what hatched the hatred! They say he quite persuaded her he was an angel of the devil. He practised spiritualism in front of her."

"Well, what if he did?"

"Don't you understand? She's so strictly religious she killed him like a fanatic. She wasn't only killing a sinner and a lecher, she was freeing the world from Antichrist! For her that was an act of merit, a religious duty! Oh, you don't know these old maids, these Old Believers! Very well then, read Dostoievski! And what Leskov wrote and Pecherski! . . . It's her, I say, it's her, even if it kills me! She smothered him! Oh, the venomous woman! Wasn't she only at the icons there, when we went in, to put us off the scent? 'I'll stand here and pray,' she said to herself, 'and they'll think I'm calm and not expecting them.' That's the way with amateur criminals. Nikolai Yermolaitch, dear friend and kinsman, give me this case! Let me see it through personally to the end! My dear friend! I've begun it and I'll see it through!"

Chubikov shook his head and frowned.

"I can deal with difficult cases on my own," he said. "It's not your job to push yourself forward. To take down what's dictated, that's your job!"

Dukovski flushed crimson, went out and slammed the door.

"He's a clever rascal!" muttered Chubikov, watching him go. "Ve—ry clever! Too much of a hothead, though. I'll have to buy him a cigar case at the fair and give it him as a present . . ."

Next morning a big-headed, hare-lipped shepherd lad called Danilka came to the examining magistrate from Klyauzov's district with some very interesting information.

"I was a bit drunk," he said. "Till midnight I stayed at my pal's. Going home, drunk as I was, I went into the river for a swim. I'm swimming there . . . then look! There's two men going along the bank and carrying something black. "Ho ho!" I shouted. They got scared and dashed off fast as they could into the Makarievski allotments. May God strike me down if it wasn't the master they were carrying!"

Before the evening of that day Psiekov and Nikolashka were arrested, taken under guard to town and put in the prison tower.

2

Twelve days passed.

It was morning and the examining magistrate, Nikolai Yermolaitch, was sitting at a green table in his house, leafing through the papers of the Klyauzov case, while Dukovski paced up and down like a restless wolf in a cage.

"You're convinced of Psiekov's guilt and Nikolashka's," he said, plucking his young beard nervously. "Why won't you be convinced of Maria Ivanovna's? Haven't you evidence enough?"

"I don't say I'm not convinced. I am but I can't somehow believe it. There's no real evidence. It's all a sort of theorizing. . . . Fanaticism and all that . . ."

"So you must have an axe and blood-stained bedclothes! You lawyer, you! Well, I'll prove it to you, then. Just drop your wishy-washy attitude to the psychological side of this. Your Maria Ivanovna should be in Siberia! I'll prove it. If theory won't do for you, I'll get something definite. . . . It'll show you how right my theory is. Just let me search around a bit."

"What are you on about?"

"That Swedish match. . . . Have you forgotten? I haven't! I'll find out who struck it in the dead man's room! Nikolashka didn't, nor Psiekov—we found no matches on them when they were searched: it was the third one, Maria Ivanovna. And I'll prove it! . . . Only let me look around the district, make inquiries . . ."

"Well, all right then. . . . Now sit down. . . . Let's get on with the questioning."

Dukovski sat down at the table and buried his long nose in the documents.

"Fetch Nikolai Tetiekhov!" shouted the examining magistrate.

Nikolashka was brought in, pale and trembling and thin as a rake.

"Tetiekhov!" Chubikov began. "In 1879 you were accused of theft and sentenced to a term of imprisonment. In 1882 you were accused a second time of theft and you went to prison again. . . . We know all about it. . . ."

Surprise came over Nikolashka's face: the omniscience of the examining magistrate amazed him. But soon surprise gave way to great distress. He sobbed and asked permission to go out and wash and calm himself. He was led out.

"Fetch Psiekov!" ordered the examining magistrate.

Psiekov was brought in. The young man's features had changed greatly in the last twelve days: he was thinner, paler, more wasted. Apathy showed in his eyes.

"Sit down, Psiekov!" said Chubikov. "I hope that you'll be reasonable today and not keep lying like the other times. For all these days you've denied your part in the murder of Klyauzov despite all the massive evidence against you. It's senseless. Confession lessens guilt. Today I'm questioning you for the last time. If you don't confess today, it will be too late tomorrow. Come on, tell us . . ."

"I know nothing. . . . And I don't know your evidence . . ." whispered Psiekov.

"That's useless! Very well, then, let me tell you how things went. On that Saturday evening you were sitting in Klyauzov's bedroom, drinking vodka and beer with him." (Dukovski fixed his eyes on Psiekov's face and kept them there through all this monologue.) "Nikolai was serving you. Between midnight and one Mark Ivanovitch told you he wanted to go to bed. He always went to bed between midnight and one. As he was taking off his boots and giving you your orders for the estate, you and Nikolai, at a given signal, grabbed your drunken master and flung him on the bed. One of you sat on his legs, the other on his head. At that moment there came in from the passage the woman in a black dress who's known to you and who had arranged with you beforehand her own part in this crime. She picked up the pillow and began to smother him with it. In the struggle the light went out. The woman took a box of Swedish matches from her pocket and lit the candle. Wasn't that the way of it? I see from your face I'm telling the truth. But to continue. . . . When you'd smothered him and were sure he was no longer breathing, you and Nikolai dragged him through the window and put him down near the burdock. Fearing he'd come round, you stabbed him with something sharp. Then you carried him and laid him down for some time under the lilac bush. You rested and thought things over, then carried him further. . . . You lifted him over a fence. . . . Then you went along the road. . . . Further on there

was the dam. Near the dam some peasant frightened you. . . .
But what's the matter with you?"

Psiekov, white as a sheet, got up and staggered about.

"I'm suffocating!" he said. "All right. . . . So be it, then. . . .
Only I must go. . . . Please. . . ."

Psiekov was taken away.

"So he's confessed at last!" said Chubikov, stretching languidly. "He gave himself away! But I handled him nicely. I
trapped him. . . ."

"And he didn't deny there was a woman in black!" chuckled
Dukovski. "But that Swedish match worries me terribly, though!
I can't stand it any longer! Goodbye! I'm off!"

Dukovski put his cap on and went out.

Chubikov began to interrogate Akulka. She declared she
knew nothing about it, nothing at all.

"I've lived only with you," she said, "and with nobody else."

At six o'clock Dukovski came back. He was more excited
than ever. His hands trembled so he couldn't undo his overcoat
and his cheeks were burning. Clearly he hadn't come back
without news.

"*Veni, vidi, vici!*" he said, leaping into Chubikov's room and
falling in a chair. "I give you my word of honour: I'm beginning
to believe in my own genius. Listen, old friend, and be amazed!
It's funny and it's sad! You've three of them in hand . . . haven't
you? I've found a fourth murderer, or rather murderess, for it's
a woman! And what a woman! For one touch of her shoulders
I'd give ten years of my life! But . . . listen. I went to Klyauzov's
village and began to circle round and round about. I called on
all the shopkeepers and innkeepers I came across and asked for
Swedish matches. Everywhere they told me no! I've been going
round till now. A dozen times I gave up hope and as many
times I got it back again. All day I've roamed about and it was
only an hour ago I found what I was looking for. Three versts
from here. They gave me a packet of ten boxes. But one box
was missing. . . . Straight off I said: "Who bought that box?"
This woman. . . . "She took a fancy to them. . . . They hiss. . . ."

Nikolai Yermolaitch, dear friend! A man expelled from a seminary
who has read Gaboriau, what he can sometimes do is quite beyond
conjecture! From this very day I shall admire myself . . . Oh
ho! . . . Well, let's be off!"

"Where to?"

"To her, the fourth one. . . . We must hurry, otherwise . . .
otherwise I'll burst with impatience! Do you know who she is?
You'll never guess! The young wife of our old Superintendent,
Yergraf Kuzmitch: Olga Petrovna, that's who! She bought that
box of matches!"

"You . . . lad . . . you . . . have you gone mad?"

"It's very clear. In the first place, she smokes. In the second,
she was head over heels in love with Klyauzov. He spurned her
love for that Akulka. Revenge! Now I remember how I found
them once, behind a screen in the kitchen. She was vowing love
to him and he was puffing one of her cigarettes and blowing
smoke into her face. But let's be off now. Hurry, it's getting
dark already. . . . Let's be off!"

"I'm not as mad as that yet: I won't disturb a respectable
gentlewoman in the evening because of what a mere boy says!"

"Respectable gentlewoman! . . . You're just a stuffed shirt,
then, not an examining magistrate! I've never dared to reprove
you before but now you force me! Stuffed shirt! Old dressing
gown! Oh, Nikolai Yermolaitch, dear friend! I implore you!"

The examining magistrate gestured angrily and spat.

"I implore you! I implore you not for myself but in the interests of justice! I'll even beg to you! Do me this favour if only
once in life!"

Dukovski fell on his knees.

"Nikolai Yermolaitch! Please be kind! Call me a scoundrel and
a rascal if I'm wrong about that woman. This is the sort of case
it is! And what a case! More like a novel than a case! The fame
of it will go through Russia! They'll make you examining magistrate for some vitally important case! Don't you realise, you
unreasonable old man!"

The examining magistrate frowned and hesitantly stretched
out his arm towards his cap.

"Oh, the devil take you!" he said. "Let's be off."

It was already dark as the examining magistrate's carriage drove up to the Superintendent's door.

"We're brutes," said Chubikov, "disturbing people like this!"

"Not to worry, not to worry. . . . Don't be scared. . . . We'll say one of our springs has broken."

A tall buxom woman of twenty-three came to greet them at the door, her eyebrows black as pitch and her lips red and full. It was Olga Petrovna herself.

"Oh . . . how nice!" she said, smiling all over her face. "You're just in time for supper. My Yergraf Kuzmitch isn't at home. . . . He's with the Father. . . . But we can do very nicely without him. . . . Come in and sit down! Are you here about a case?"

"Well, yes. . . . But one of our springs is broken, you see . . ." said Chubikov, going into the drawing room and sitting down in an easy-chair.

"Now, at once . . ." whispered Dukovski, ". . . give her a shock! A shock!"

"A spring . . . you see . . . H'm. . . . We stopped and called."

"Shock her, I said! She'll guess if you spin it out!"

"Oh, do as you like, but leave me be!" muttered Chubikov, getting up and going to the window. "I can't do it! You've made the mess, eat it!"

"Yes, the spring . . ." began Dukovski, going up to the Superintendent's wife and wrinkling his long nose, "we . . . didn't come here for . . . er . . . er . . . supper nor to see Yergraf Kuzmitch. We came, in fact, to ask you the whereabouts of Mark Ivanovitch, whom you murdered."

"What? What Mark Ivanovitch?" murmured the Superintendent's wife, and suddenly, in a moment, her full face flushed crimson. "I . . . I don't understand . . ."

"Answer in the name of the law! Where's Klyauzov? We know all about it."

"From whom?" she asked quietly, unable to bear Dukovski's stare.

"Kindly inform us where he is!"

"But how do you know? Who told you?"

"We know all about it! I demand an answer in the name of the law!"

Prompted by her confusion, the examining magistrate went up to her and said:

"Tell us and we'll go. . . . But otherwise . . ."

"What do you want with him?"

"What's the point of these questions, Madam? We want information from you. You're trembling, confused. . . . Yes, he's been killed: if you like, killed by you! Your accomplices have given you away!"

The Superintendent's wife went pale.

"Come . . ." she said quietly, wringing her hands. "He's hidden in my bath-house. Only, for God's sake, don't tell my husband. I beg you. He won't be able to stand it."

The Superintendent's wife took a big key from the wall and led them through the kitchen and a corridor into the courtyard. It was dark there. A drizzle of rain was falling. She led the way and Chubikov and Dukovski followed over deep grass, breathing the smells of wild hemp and slops that squelched under their feet. It was a big courtyard. Soon they were past the slop puddles and their feet felt ploughed ground. Silhouettes of trees showed in the darkness and among them a little house with a crooked chimney.

"That's the bath-house!" said the Superintendent's wife. "But I beg you, don't tell anybody!"

When they reached the bath-house, Chubikov and Dukovski saw a huge padlock on the door.

"Get your bit of candle ready and the matches!" whispered the examining magistrate to his assistant.

The Superintendent's wife undid the lock and let them into the bath-house. Dukovski struck a match and lit up the changing-room. In the middle there was a fat little samovar on a table, beside it a tureen with cold soup and a dish with remains of sausage.

"Go ahead!"

They went into the next room, the bath-house itself. A table was there too with a big dish of ham, a bottle of vodka, plates and knives and forks.

"But where . . . where is he, then? Where's the corpse?" asked the examining magistrate.

"He's on the top shelf!" whispered the Superintendent's wife, still trembling all over and pale.

Dukovski took the little candle and climbed to the top shelf. There he saw the long body of a man, lying motionless on a big feather mattress. From it came a faint snore. . . .

"They've fooled us, blast it!" shouted Dukovski. "This isn't him! This idiot lying here's alive! Oh! Who are you, curse you?"

The body wheezed as it drew in air and moved. Dukovski prodded it with his elbow. It put its hands up, stretched itself and lifted its head.

"Who's that poking?" asked a deep, hoarse voice. "What do you want?"

Dukovski held the little candle to the stranger's face and gave a shriek. In the red nose, tousled, uncombed hair and black-as-pitch moustache, one tip jauntily turned up and pointing saucily at the ceiling, he recognized Klyauzov, retired guard's officer.

"You. . . . Mark . . . Ivanovitch? It can't be!"

The examining magistrate looked up and went stiff with amazement. . . .

"Yes, it's me. . . . Why, it's you, Dukovski! What the devil do you want here? And who's that ugly mug down there? God, the examining magistrate! Well I never!"

Klyauzov climbed down and embraced Chubikov. Olga Petrovna slipped through the door.

"How did you get here? Let's have a drink, curse it! Tra-la-la-la-la-la. . . . Let's drink! Who brought you here, though? How did you know I was here? It's all the same, though! Drink!"

Klyauzov lit the lamp and poured out three glasses of vodka.

"The fact is . . . I don't understand you," said the examining magistrate, thrusting out his hands. "Is it you or isn't it?"

"Now stop it! . . . To read me a lesson, is that what you're after? Don't bother! Drink your glass, young Dukovski! Let it all go, friends. . . . What are you staring for? Drink!"

"All the same I can't understand," said the examining magistrate, mechanically drinking his vodka. "Why are you here?"

"And why shouldn't I be here, if I feel good here?"

Klyauzov drank and ate some ham.

"I'm living with the Superintendent's wife, as you can see. In the woods and thickets like a house goblin. Drink! I got sorry for her, brother. I felt sorry and, well, I'm living here in this secluded bath-house like a hermit. . . . I feed well. . . . But I'm thinking of clearing off next week. . . . It's boring me. . . ."

"Incredible!" said Dukovski.

"And what's incredible about it?"

"Incredible! How did your boot get into the garden, for God's sake?"

"What boot?"

"We found one boot in the bedroom and the other in the garden."

"Well, what do you want to know for? It's not your affair. . . . Go on, drink, curse you! You woke me up, so drink! It's an interesting story, brothers, what happened with the boot. I didn't want to go to Olga. Not in the mood, you know. . . . I was under the influence. . . . She came outside the window and started nagging. . . . You know what women are. . . . Mostly. . . . I was drunk and I got my boot and flung it at her. . . . Ha ha! Don't nag, I said! She climbed through the window, lit the lamp and spanked me, drunk as I was. She gave me a hiding, dragged me here and locked me in. Now she feeds me up. . . . Love, vodka and tidbits! But where are you going? Chubikov, where are you off to?"

The examining magistrate spat and went out of the bathhouse. Dukovski followed him, head bowed. They sat down quietly in the carriage and drove off. Never had the road seemed so dull and long as now. Both were silent. Chubikov was trembling with fury all the way and Dukovski buried his face in

44

his collar as if afraid the dark and drizzle would read shame there.

When the examining magistrate reached home, he found Doctor Tutuiev in the house. He was sitting at the table, sighing deeply as he turned the pages of the *Neva*.

"The things that go on in this world!" he said, greeting Chubikov with a sad smile. "Austria's at it again! . . . And Gladstone too, in a way. . . ."

Chubikov flung his hat under the table and began to shake.

"Don't pester me, you evil skeleton! I've told you a thousand times not to pester me with your politics. This is no time for politics! And as for you. . . ." He turned on Dukovski and shook his fist. "As for you . . . I'll not forget this in ten thousand years!"

"But . . . that Swedish match! How was I to know?"

"Go choke yourself with your match! Be off and stop annoying me or the devil knows what I'll do to you! Don't put a foot inside this door!"

Dukovski sighed, took his cap and went out.

"I'll go and get drunk!" he decided, coming out of the gate, and sauntering sadly towards the tavern.

When the Superintendent's wife came in from the bathhouse, she found her husband in the drawing room.

"What did the Superintendent come for?" he asked.

"He came to say they've found Klyauzov. Fancy, they found him with another man's wife!"

"Ah, Mark Ivanovitch, Mark Ivanovitch!" sighed the Superintendent, looking upwards. "I told you: no good comes of debauchery! I told you—but you wouldn't listen!"

Tears the World Does Not See
1884

"NOW, NOBLE GENTLEMEN, it wouldn't be a bad idea to have a little supper," said Lieutenant Colonel Rebrotyesov, garrison commander, tall and thin as a telegraph pole, as he came out of the club with his friends one dark August night. "In first rate cities, like Saratov, say, you can always have supper in the club, but in this stinking Chervyanska of ours, apart from vodka and tea with flies in it, there isn't a thing to be had. Drinking with not a morsel to eat is worse than nothing."

"Yes, it wouldn't be a bad idea to have a little something now," agreed Ivan Ivanitch Dvoetochiev, inspector of ecclesiastical schools, muffling himself from the wind in his rust-coloured overcoat. "It's two o'clock already and the taverns are shut but some herrings wouldn't be a bad idea . . . or mushrooms, say . . . or something of the sort, you know. . . ."

He waggled his fingers in the air and sketched a sort of dish across his face, a very savoury one, no doubt, for everybody looking licked their lips. The group came to a halt and began thinking. They thought and thought but couldn't think up anything to eat: they had to confine themselves only to dreams.

"At Golopesov's one splendid evening I ate turkey!" sighed Prujina-Prujinski, Assistant Police Commissioner. "By the way . . . you were in Warsaw some time or other, weren't you, gentlemen? They do this there. . . . They take ordinary carp, alive . . . and frisky and put 'em in milk. . . . For a day the things swim about in milk and then they fry them in sour cream in the pan

46

just so . . . that then, my friend, you can keep your pineapples! My God! Especially if you drink a glass and then another. You eat . . . in a sort of oblivion. You can't feel it. . . . Just from the aroma you could die!"

"And if you've salted cucumbers too . . ." added Rebrotyesov with heartfelt fellow-feeling. "When we were stationed in Poland . . . we used to have those meat dumplings two hundred at a time in a stew. . . . You'd a full plateful of them, shook on pepper, strewed fennel and parsley. . . . There's no word to describe it!"

Suddenly Rebrotyesov stopped and was pensive. There came to his mind a dish of sturgeon that he ate in 1856 at the Triatska Monastery. So savoury was his memory of that sturgeon that the garrison commander sniffed suddenly the smell of fish and chewed unconsciously, not noticing that mud was gathering in his galoshes.

"No, no!" He said. "I can't stand it any longer! I'm going home to satisfy my appetite. I'll tell you what, gentlemen, you come to my place, too. Yes, by God! We'll drink our glass and eat whatever God provides. Cucumber, sausage. . . . We'll set up the samovar. . . . What about it? we'll eat, we'll chat about the plague, we'll remember old times. . . . My wife's asleep but we won't go and wake her. . . . Quietly then. . . . Come on!"

There is no need to describe the enthusiasm with which the invitation was received. I will only say that never was such good will shown to Rebrotyesov as on that night.

"I'll box your ears!" said the garrison commander to his batman as he led his guests into the dark hall. "I've told you a thousand times, you scoundrel, to burn sweet-smelling tissues when you sleep in the hall. Go and set up the samovar, you idiot, and tell Irina she'd better bring . . . some cucumber and radish from the larder. . . . Yes, and prepare some herrings. . . . Crumble some spring onions with them, yes, and strew fennel . . . you know . . . and slice potatoes in a circle round. . . . And beetroot too. . . . All together, you know, with vinegar and butter and mustard. . . . Sprinkle pepper over it. . . . Garnish, in fact. . . . Understand?"

47

Rebrotyesov waddled his fingers to describe the concoction, garnishing in mime what he could not garnish in words. His guests took off their galoshes and went into a dark room. The master of the house struck a match, diffusing sulphur, and lit up walls decked with prizes from *Neva*,* views of Venice and portraits of the writer Lajechnikov and a certain general with astonished eyes.

"In no time at all . . ." whispered Rebrotyesov, quietly taking up the table cover, ". . . I'll lay the table and we'll be seated. . . . My Masha was rather sick today. . . . Please excuse her. . . . One of these women's things. . . . Dr. Goosin says it's from the lenten fare she eats. . . . May well be! 'Darling,' I tell her, 'it's not a question of food. Not what goes in your mouth,' I say, 'but what comes out.' 'You eat lenten fare,' I tell her, 'and get upset as usual.' 'Instead of mortifying your flesh,' I say, 'better cheer up and stop complaining.' She won't listen! 'From childhood,' she says, 'this has been our discipline.'"

The batman came in and, craning his neck, whispered something in his master's ear. Rebrotyesov raised his eyebrows.

"Ah yes . . ." he murmured. "H'm. . . . That so. . . . But it's nothing, though. . . . I'll put that right in a minute. Masha, don't you see, has locked the larder and the cupboards to keep the servants out and she has the keys. I'll have to go and get them. . . ."

Rebrotyesov rose on tiptoe, quietly opened the door and went to his wife. She was asleep.

"Manechka," he said, stealthily approaching the bed, "Manechka, wake up a second."

"Who's there? You, is it? What do you want?"

"Manechka, here's what I'm about. . . . Give me the keys, angel, and don't disturb yourself. . . . Go on sleeping. . . . I'll take care of them. . . . I'll give them some cucumber and use up nothing more. . . . In God's name! There's Dvoetochiev, you know, Prujina-Prujinski and a few more. . . . All splendid people. . . . Important socially. . . . Prujinski has the order of Vladimir, even, fourth class. . . . He's a high regard for you. . . ."

* A newspaper.

"Where've you been slobbering?"

"Now then, you're getting angry already. . . . You're like that, it's true. . . . I'll give them cucumber, that'll be all. . . . And they'll go. . . . I'll take charge of everything and not disturb you. . . . Stay in bed, my little doll. . . . And how are you feeling now? Was Dr. Goosin here without me? There, I kiss your hand, see. . . . And the guests have such a high regard for you. . . . Dvoetochiev is a devout man, you know. . . . Prujina is paymaster too. . . . They all think a lot of you. . . . 'Maria,' they say, 'Maria Patrovna, she's not just a lady,' they say, 'but something quite wonderful . . . the high light of our society.' "

"Come to bed and stop your fussing! Slobbering with your cronies at the club and then blabbering all night! You ought to be ashamed! You have children!"

"Yes . . . I have children, but don't upset yourself, Manechka . . . don't grieve. . . . I embrace and love you. . . . And the children, God knows, I'm attached to them. I take Mitya to the high school, don't I? . . . I couldn't have done more to send them packing. . . . It's awkward. . . . They followed me and asked for food. 'Give us something to eat,' they said. Dvoetochiev, Prujina-Prujinski . . . such nice people. . . . They're fond of you, they appreciate you. Give them some cucumber and a drink . . . and be content. . . . I'll take charge. . . ."

"Oh, the torment of it! Have you gone crazy or what? Guests like that at this time? They ought to be ashamed, the devil take them, disturbing people at night! Where in the world do you see guests turning up at night? Aren't there taverns here for them? I'd be an idiot giving you the keys. Let them go and have a sleep and come back tomorrow."

"H'm. . . . You would say that. . . . But I won't abase myself before you. . . . It's clear and plain you're not the comfort of your husband, the lifelong friend of which the Scriptures speak. . . . It's disgustingly evident. . . . You were a little viper and you are still!"

"Ah! So you can abuse me still, can you, pest that you are?"

"*Merci*. . . . I read the truth once in one of the papers: 'Among other people she's an angel, not a woman, but at home with her husband, a she-devil.' It's the solemn truth. . . . You were a devil and you're a devil still. . . ."

"Take that, you!"

"Go on, go on! Beat your own husband! Well, I'll get down on my knees and beg to you. . . . I implore you, Manechka! Forgive me! . . . Give me the keys! Manechka! Angel! Don't put me to shame before society! My wild barbarian woman, how long will you torment me? Go on. . . . Beat me. . . . *Merci.* . . . I'll entreat you just the same!"

The married couple conversed a long time in this fashion. Rebrotyesov got down on his knees, twice burst into tears, railed at himself and kept scratching his cheek. . . . It ended when his wife got up, spat and said:

"I see there's going to be no end to my torment! Give me my dress from the chair, Mahomet!"

Rebrotyesov carefully passed her the dress and, setting his hair in place, went to his guests. They were standing in front of the general's portrait, staring at his astonished eyes, and debating the question which was the elder, the general or the writer. Dvoetochiev took the part of Lajechnikov, the writer, urging his immortality. Prujinski, however, said:

"The man's a writer. Let's say a good one, we won't argue. And he writes with humour and sympathy. But send him off to war and he can't cope there with the troops. Yet give a general a full army corps, why, it's nothing to him. . . ."

"My Masha will be here right away . . ." said Rebrotyesov, coming in and interrupting the discussion. "Just a minute. . . ."

"We're putting you to trouble, aren't we? . . . Fedor Akimitch, what's the matter with your cheek? My dear chap, you've a black eye! Where did you land yourself with that?"

"My cheek? Where on my cheek?" muttered Rebrotyesov in confusion. "Ah yes! I sneaked in to Manechka just now, I wanted to give her a fright and all of a sudden in the darkness I bumped into the bed. Ha ha! . . . But here is Manechka. . . . What a tousle-head you look, Manechka mine! A real Louise Michell"

Maria Petrovna came into the dining room, tousled and sleepy but radiant and cheerful.

"How kind of you to call!" she said. "If you couldn't come by day, then thank my husband for bringing you at any rate by night. I was asleep just now and heard a voice. . . . Who could it be? I thought. . . . Fedor wanted me to stay in bed and not come out to you, but, well, I couldn't resist. . . ."

She hurried out to the kitchen and the supper began. . . .

"How wonderful to be married!" sighed Prujina-Prujinski, leaving the garrison commander's house an hour later with the others. "You eat when you like and drink when you feel like it. . . . You know there's a fellow creature who loves you. . . . And plays something for you on the piano. . . . Rebrotyesov's a happy man!"

Dvoetochiev was silent. He sighed and brooded. When he arrived home and was undressing, he sighed so loudly that he woke his wife.

"Don't make such a row with your boots, you oaf!" said his wife. "You won't let a person sleep. Gallivanting at the club and then making this racket! You're a fine specimen!"

"All you know is how to quarrel!" moaned the inspector of schools. "You ought to see how Rebrotyesov and his wife live! By God, they do live! Watch them and you feel like weeping, it's so endearing. My only misery is that you've been born on this earth to torment me. Move over!"

The inspector of schools covered himself with the quilt and, brooding on his fate, fell asleep.

Ninotchka
1885

T HE DOOR quietly opened and my good friend Pavel
Sergeivitch Vikhlienev came in to see me, young in years
but looking old and sick. He was droop-shouldered, long-nosed
and skinny, everything about him ugly, yet his features were
so open, so soft and so diffuse that every time I gazed on them
a strange wish came to take them in five fingers and feel there,
as it were, all the soft-heartedness and flabby sincerity of my
friend. Like all unpractical people he was quiet, timid and bash-
ful but this time he was pale too and deeply worried about
something.

"What's the matter?" I asked, taking a long look at his pale
face and lightly trembling lips. "Are you ill, is that it, or have
you had another tiff with your wife? You seem in a bad way."

Fumbling a little and coughing, Vikhlienev flapped his hand.

"It's Ninotchka again," he said. "Trouble! So painful, my
dear chap, that all night long I couldn't sleep and now, as
you see, I'm more dead than alive. . . . The Devil's down on me.
You don't find other people with such trouble. They bear things
lightly, insults, loss and illness but for me a mere trifle's enough
and I'm limp and exhausted."

"But what's happened?"

"Trivial things. A little domestic fuss. . . . Well, I'll tell you,
if you like. Yesterday evening my Ninotchka didn't go out
anywhere, she stayed at home and wanted to spend the evening
with me. I was very glad, of course. She usually goes out to

52

some gathering or other in the evening and as it's only evenings I'm at home you can judge how very . . . very glad I was. But then you've never been married so you can't realize how warm-hearted and cosy you feel coming home from work to find there what you live for. . . . Ah!"

Vikhlienev described the charms of family life, wiped the sweat from his brow and went on:

"Ninotchka felt like a nice little evening with me. But you know what I'm like, don't you? A dull chap, boring, no sparkle. What fun is there with me? Always with my drawings and my filter and sand. I don't play games, I don't dance, I don't make jokes. I'm not cut out for that, but Ninotchka, you must admit, she's young and fresh. And youth has its rights . . . hasn't it?

"Well, I started to show her pictures, different kinds of little articles and whatnot . . . told her things. And then I happened to remember there were some old letters in my table with some very funny stuff in them. Some friends in my student days wrote very cunningly and craftily. You read and split your sides! I pulled out the letters from the table and began to read them to Ninotchka. I read one, two, three . . . then everything came to a halt. In one letter, you see, there was this phrase: 'Katya sends her love!' A phrase like that . . . it's like a knife into a jealous wife and my Ninotchka is an Othello in skirts. The questions that beat down on my wretched head! 'Who's this little Katya of yours? What's she like? What's she to you?' I told her that little Katya . . . well, it was a case of first love, something young and green and adolescent, scarcely worth consideration. Every young man, I told her, has his little Katya, it's bound to happen. . . .

"My Ninotchka wouldn't listen. She imagined the devil knows what and burst into tears. And after tears came hysteria: 'You scoundrel!' she shouted. 'Swine! So you've a Katya even now of some sort, you're hiding her, that's what you're doing!'"

"I reassured her, yes, I reassured her . . . but what was the good? Masculine logic never works with women. In the end I asked forgiveness on my knees. . . . I grovelled and I don't know what. And she went to bed in hysterics: all by herself, and me all by myself on the sofa. . . . This morning she didn't look at me, she sulked and stared about. She swears she's going back to her mother. And believe me, she'll go, I know her character!"

"'Dear me, what a sad story!"

"Women are incomprehensible to me. But let's admit it, Ninotchka is young and strict and fastidious . . . a worldly affair like my little Katya is bound to annoy her . . . but is it really hard to forgive? All right, I did wrong, but then I asked forgiveness. I grovelled on my knees! And, if you really want to know, . . . I even cried!"

"Yes, women are a mystery!"

"My dear chap, you've a big influence on Ninotchka: she respects you as an authority. I beg you, call and see her, exert that influence on her, all of it, and convince her what a mistake she's making. I'm suffering, old chap! If it's the same story again today, I shan't be able to bear it. Call and see her, dear fellow."

"But won't it be embarrassing?"

"Why embarrassing? Why? You've been her friend almost from childhood. She trusts you. Call and see her. Be a good chap!"

Vikhlienev's tearful pleading touched me. I got dressed and went to see his wife.

I found Ninotchka at her favorite pastime: crossing her legs on the sofa, gazing into the air with her pretty screwed-up eyes and doing nothing. As she saw me, she jumped from the sofa and ran to me. . . . Then she looked about her, quickly closed the door and light as a feather put her arms around my neck. (The reader need suspect no printer's error here: for a year or more I've shared with Vikhlienev his conjugal rights.)

"And what have you been up to this time, sly one?" I asked her, sitting her beside me.

"What do you mean?"

"You've thought up another torture for your better half. Yes, he came to me today and told me all about his little Katya."

"Oh? Is that so? He's found someone to tell his sorrows to!"

"What happened between you?"

"You know, nothing really. . . . Last night it was so boring.

54

It made me spiteful because I'd nowhere to go and so in my annoyance I nagged at him about his little Katya. It was boredom I was crying with but how do you explain a thing like that to him?"

"But all the same, my love, it's cruel and inhuman. He's so overwrought and still you plague him with your scenes."

"Not at all! He loves it when I'm jealous. . . . And there's nothing like pretended jealousy to keep him from suspecting. But stop talking like this. I don't like it when you start talking about my milksop of a husband. . . . Oh, he bores me so! Let's have some tea, that's better. . . ."

"All the same you must stop torturing him. . . . It's pitiful to see him, you know. . . . He talks so frankly and sincerely about his family happiness and is so sure of your love it becomes painful to listen. . . . You must control yourself somehow: snuggle up to him and tell white lies. Just a single word from you could put him in the seventh heaven."

Ninotchka pouted and frowned but nevertheless when Vikhlienev came in a little later and glanced timidly at me, she gave him a cheerful smile and looked at him with tenderness.

"You're just in time for tea," she told him. "There's my clever fellow, never late. . . . Cream for you, is it, or lemon?"

Not expecting such a greeting, Vikhlienev was deeply moved. He kissed his wife's arm tenderly and embraced me and it was so absurd, this embrace, and so unexpected that both of us blushed, Ninotchka and I.

"Blessed are the Peacemakers!" clucked the happy husband. "So you managed to convince her. And why? Because you're a man of the world, you move in the right circles, you know all the subtleties of a woman's heart! Ha! Ha! Ha! But I'm a clumsy oaf! One word needed and I say ten. . . . To kiss her hand or something, that's what's needed, but I start moaning! Ha! Ha! Ha!"

After the tea Vikhlienev took me into his study, buttonholed me there and mumbled:

"I don't know how to thank you, my dear fellow. You know, I was suffering so much, I was in torment, and now I'm so happy it's more than I can take! And it's not the first time you've got me out of a horrible situation. My dear friend, don't deny me this. There's one little thing that's mine . . . really it's a tiny locomotive that I made myself. . . . I got a medal for it at an exhibition. . . . Take it . . . in friendship . . . as a token of my gratitude! Do me that favour!"

Of course I made every possible excuse but Vikhlienev was adamant and there was nothing for it but to take his precious gift.

Days passed, weeks, months . . . and inevitably with time the cursed truth was revealed to Vikhlienev in all its sordid splendour. When by accident he came to know it, he turned terribly pale, lay down on the sofa and stared stupidly at the ceiling. . . . He didn't speak a single word but then, mental anguish forced somehow into movement, he tossed and turned tormentedly, his weak nature permitting only this reaction.

A week later, somewhat recovered from his devastating shock, Vikhlienev came to see me. We were both embarrassed and did not look at one another. Quite to no purpose I began to babble about free love, the egotism of a husband and resignation to one's fate.

"I'm not here . . . for that . . ." he interrupted meekly. "I understand all that quite perfectly. No one is to blame for his feelings. It's another aspect of the matter that concerns me, something quite practical. My dear man, I know so little of life and when it's a question of manners and social arrangement I'm all at sea. You can help me, dear friend. Advise me now what Ninotchka's mode of life should be. Should she go on living with me or do you think it preferable she come to you?"

We deliberated briefly and came to this decision: Ninotchka is to go on living with Vikhlienev and I visit her whenever I feel like it; and then Vikhlienev takes himself off to a corner room, previously used as a store. It's a little damp and dark, this room, and the way to it is through a kitchen, but he can shut himself up there quite completely and offend the eye of no one.

56

Nerves
1885

DIMITRI OSIPOVITCH VAKSIN, the architect, returned
to his *dacha* from town with the impact of his experiences
at a spiritualist seance still fresh upon him. Undressing and getting into his solitary bed—Madam Vaksin had gone out to an
all-night Trinity service—Vaksin began despite himself to remember all he had seen and heard.

It wasn't, strictly speaking, a seance, for the evening went by
with nothing but frightening talk. Some lady, for no particular
reason, started talking about telepathy; from that they passed
imperceptibly to spirits, from spirits to ghosts, and from ghosts
to the buried alive. . . . Some gentleman read out a terrible
tale about a corpse that turned in its coffin. Then Vaksin himself
called for a saucer and showed a young lady how to get in touch
with spirits. He summoned his uncle, as it happened, Klavdi
Mironovitch, and asked him by mental contact: "Isn't it time
I transferred my house to my wife's name?" To which Uncle
replied: "All things are good in the blessing of time."

"So much in nature . . . is mysterious and terrible. . . ." brooded
Vaksin, lying down under the blanket. "The dead are not terrible, it's the unknown . . ."

It struck one. Vaksin turned over and peeped from under the
blanket at the little blue light of the icon-lamp. It twinkled only
just enough to light the icon and the big portrait of Uncle Klavdi
Mironovitch hanging opposite the bed.

57

"What if uncle's spirit appeared here and now in the dark?" flashed into Vaksin's mind. "No, that's impossible!"

Ghosts—they are mere superstition bred in immature minds; but all the same Vaksin pulled the blanket over his head and shut his eyes tighter. In his imagination gleamed a dead body turning over in its coffin and there came along the ghosts of his late mother-in-law, a colleague who hanged himself and a girl who was drowned. . . . Vaksin strove to drive the dark thoughts from his mind but the harder he strove, the more fearful they were and the visions were clearer. It terrified him.

"Oh the devil! Scaring myself like a little boy! This is stupid!"

"Tick, tick, tick," tapped the clock on the wall. From the village church in the cemetery came a peal, slow, mournful and poignant. . . . A cold shiver ran over Vaksin's neck and down his back and someone seemed to breathe heavily over his head as if uncle had come out of the frame and were leaning over his nephew. . . .

Vaksin became unbearably frightened. He clenched his teeth in terror and held his breath. And at last, as a beetle flew in at the open window and droned over his bed, he could stand no more and desperately pulled the bell.

"Dmitri Osipovitch, *was wollen Sie?*" came a minute later the voice of the governess outside the door.

"Oh, it's you, Rosalie Karlovna?" said Vaksin with delight. "But why did you trouble? Couldn't Gabriella . . . ?"

"Gabriella you yourself to town sent, and the Countess somewhere in the evening went out. Nobody at home at all . . . *Was wollen Sie doch?*"

"Well, my dear, this is what I wanted to say. . . . In fact . . . But come in, don't be shy! I'm in the dark. . . ."

Rosalie Karlovna, plump and rosy-cheeked, came into the bedroom and stood waiting.

"Sit down, dear . . . You see, the fact of the matter. . . ."

Whatever can I ask her? wondered Vaksin, squinting at uncle's portrait and feeling his mood come gradually to calm.

"Actually, this is what I wanted to ask you. . . . When the man sets off for town tomorrow, don't forget to tell him . . . to . . .

call and buy cigarette papers. . . . Do sit down!"

"Cigarette papers. All right. *Was wollen Sie noch?*"

"*Ich will.* There's nothing *Ich will* but. . . . Do sit down! I'll think of something yet. . . ."

"It's not decent for a girl to be in a man's bedroom. You, I see, Dimitri Osipovitch, are a mischievous man . . . playing pranks . . . I know. . . . For cigarette papers a person you do not wake up. . . . I know. . . ."

Rosalie Karlovna turned round and went out. Rather comforted by talking to her and ashamed of being a coward, Vaksin pulled the blanket over his head and shut his eyes. For ten minutes he felt all right but then that silly nonsense crept into his head again. He cleared his throat, felt for the matches and, without opening his eyes, lit a candle. But the light didn't help. In his jittery state he felt someone was peering at him from a corner and that uncle's eyes blinked.

"I'll ring for her again, damn her!" he decided. "I'll tell her I'm ill. I'll ask for some drops."

Vaksin rang. There was no response. He rang again and like an echo there came a peal from the cemetery. Terror-stricken, cold all over, he bounded out of the bedroom, then crossed himself, cursing his cowardice, and scampered, barefoot and in nothing but a shirt, to Rosalie's room.

"Rosalie Karlovna," he began, his voice trembling as he beat upon the door. "Rosalie Karlovna! Are you . . . asleep? I'm . . . h'm . . . ill . . . Drops!"

There was no response. All round was silence.

"I'm begging you. . . . You understand? Begging you! Why all this standing on ceremony, I don't understand it, especially when a man's ill? . . . You're giving yourself airs and graces and no mistake. At your age. . . ."

"I your wife shall tell. . . . Will not leave in peace a respectable girl. . . . When I was with Baron Enzig and the baron wanted to come to me for matches, I know. . . . I straightaway know, what sort of matches . . . and I told the baroness. . . . I'm a respectable girl. . . ."

"Oh, what the devil has your respectability to do with me?

I'm ill . . . and I'm begging you for drops. Do you understand? I'm ill!"

"Your wife is respectable, good woman, and you ought her to love. *Ja!* She is a noble person! I not wish to be her enemy!"

"You're an idiot, that's all! Understand? An idiot!"

Vaksin leaned against the doorpost, folded his arms and waited for his fears to leave him.

To return to his room where the icon-lamp twinkled and uncle stared out of his portrait, no, he hadn't the strength, yet to stand at the governess's door in only a nightshirt was awkward however you looked at it. What was he to do?

It struck two; and his dread was not gone yet nor decreased. It was dark in the corridor and something dark seemed to peer from every corner. Vaksin turned his face to the doorpost but at once someone seemed to tug at his shirt from behind and touch his shoulder. . . .

"The devil take it. . . . Rosalie Karlovna!"

There was no response. Timidly Vaksin opened the door and peeped into the room. The virtuous Fraulein was sleeping peacefully and a little nightlight lit the outlines of her plump, sturdily-breathing body. Vaksin came into the room and sat down on a wicker trunk near the door. In the presence of someone sleeping yet alive he felt better.

"Let her sleep, the German fool . . ." he thought. "I'll sit here in her room and go when it's light. . . . It gets light early these days."

Vaksin stretched out on the trunk to wait for dawn, put his hands under his head and began to ponder.

"What do nerves mean anyway? An intelligent man, a thinker, and at the same time . . . the devil knows what! Ought to be ashamed even. . . ."

But soon, listening to Rosalie Karlovna's soft and regular breathing, he recovered altogether. . . .

At six o'clock in the morning Vaksin's wife came back from the Trinity service, and, when she couldn't find her husband in the bedroom, came to the governess's room to ask her for some change to pay the coachman. As she entered, a strange sight met her eyes: Rosalie Karlovna sleeping, spreadeagled on the bed for the heat, and a couple of yards off, on a wicker trunk, curled up snoring in the sleep of the just, her husband, barefoot and in only a nightshirt.

What she said and her husband's inane look as he awoke I leave others to describe. I am quite helpless and give up the struggle.

The Boots
1885

M IRKIN, THE PIANO-TUNER, clean-shaven, with yellow face, tobacco-stained nose and cotton wool in his ears, came out into the corridor, calling plaintively.

"Simeon! Boots!"

And you might have thought from his frightened face that the plaster had fallen on him or he'd just seen a ghost in his room.

"Simeon, for pity's sake!" he cried, seeing the boots come running. "What's all this then? I suffer from rheumatism, I'm a sick man, and you're forcing me to go out barefoot! Why haven't you given me my boots by this time? Where are they?"

Simeon went into Mirkin's room, looked where he usually put the finished boots and scratched his head. The boots weren't there.

"Now where are they, cursed things?" said Simeon. "Seems last night I cleaned them and put them there. . . . H'm. . . . Yesterday I was tight, I must admit. I dare say I must have put them in another room. That must be it, Afanasi Yegoritch, in another room. There's such a lot of boots and the devil mixes them up in the sight of a drunken man, if you're not careful. . . . I must have put them in the lady next door's . . . the actress . . ."

"Now I have to go and disturb a lady, if you please, because of you! Because of this nonsense, if you please, I have to wake up a respectable woman!"

Sighing and coughing, Mirkin went to the door of the next room and carefully knocked.

"Who's there?" came a woman's voice a moment later.

"It is *I!*" began Mirkin plaintively, like an admirer addressing a lady of fashion. "Pardon me for disturbing you, Madam, but I'm a sick man, I suffer from rheumatism. Madam, my doctors have instructed me to keep my feet warm, especially as I must go at once to tune the piano for the wife of General Shevelitzin. But I can't go to her barefoot!"

"But what is it you want? What piano?"

"Not a piano, Madam. It's a matter of boots! That idiot Simeon cleaned mine and put them in your room by mistake. Madam, be so kind as to give me my boots!"

He heard a rustling, a jump from bed and a slithering of slippers, then the door opened a little and a fat, feminine hand flung a pair of boots at Mirkin's feet. The piano-tuner expressed his thanks and went back to his room.

"Funny . . ." he muttered, putting on a boot. "Seems as if it's not the right boot. Yes, there are two left boots! Both left boots! Simeon, do you hear, these are not my boots. My boots have red tabs and no patches and these are torn and haven't tabs!"

Simeon picked up the boots, turned them over once or twice in front of his eyes and frowned.

"They're Pavel Alexandrovitch's boots. . . ," he muttered with a sidelong look.

He had a squint in his left eye.

"What Pavel Alexandrovitch?"

"The actor. . . . Comes here every Tuesday. . . . He must have put yours on instead of his. . . . I must have taken both pairs to her room: yours and his. Commission!"

"Then go and change them!"

"Fine how-do-you do!" chuckled Simeon. "Go and change them! . . . And where am I to get him now? An hour he's been gone. . . . Go chase the wind in the fields!"

"Where's he live, then?"

"But who knows? He comes here every Tuesday but as for where he lives . . . unknown. He comes, spends the night . . . then wait till next Tuesday. . . ."

"See what you've done, you lout! Well, what am I to do now!

It's time for me to go to General Shevelitzin's wife, you reprobate! My feet will freeze!"

"It doesn't take long to change a pair of boots. Put these on, wear them till evening, and in the evening go to the theatre. . . . Ask there for Blistanov, the actor. . . . If you don't want to go to the theatre, then you'll have to wait till Tuesday. He only comes here on Tuesdays. . . ."

"But why are there two left boots?" asked the piano-tuner, regarding them with wary distaste.

"What God sends, we have to bear. Because we're poor. . . . Where are you to find that actor? . . . 'Pavel Alexandrovitch,' I say, 'these boots of yours! Disgraceful!' 'Tremble and look pale!' he says. 'In these very boots,' he says, 'have I played counts and princes.' Queer people! In a word, artists. If I were governor or some big official, I'd get all these actors . . . and put them in prison."

Groaning and scowling Mirkin pulled the two left boots on his feet and limped his way to the house of General Shevelitzin's wife. All day he walked about the town to tune pianos and all day fancied everyone was looking at his feet, seeing his boots had patches and were down at heel. Besides his mental agony there came another, physical, to try him: he got a corn.

In the evening he was at the theatre. They were playing *Bluebeard*. Just before the last act, helped by a flautist he knew, he went back stage. Going into the men's dressing room, he found all the male actors in the company there. One was changing, another making up, a third smoking. Bluebeard was standing with King Bobesh and showing him a revolver.

"Buy it!" he said. "I bought it myself in Kursk for eight, as it happens; well, I'll let you have it for six. . . . Marvellous action!"

"Careful. . . . It's loaded!"

"May I see Mr. Blistanov?" asked the piano-tuner as he came in.

"I'm the man himself!"—Bluebeard turned to him.—"What can I do for you?"

"Please excuse me, sir, if I disturb you," pleaded the piano-tuner, "but believe me, I'm a sick man, I suffer from rheumatism. My doctors have instructed me to keep my feet warm . . ."

"But what, in fact, can I do for you?"

"Well, you see," went on the piano-tuner directly to Bluebeard, ". . . the fact is . . . last night you found yourself in Bukteev's boarding house . . . in room sixty-four . . ."

"Now then, what's all this?" chuckled King Bobesh. "My wife lives in room sixty-four!"

"Your wife? How very nice! . . ." Mirkin smiled. "She then, your wife, in fact, handed me these boots. When he"—he pointed to Bluebeard—"went away from her, I missed my boots. . . . I shouted, you see, for the boots but the boots said: 'But, sir, I put your boots in the next room!' By mistake, when he was drunk, he put in room sixty-four my boots and yours as well. . . ." —Mirkin turned to Blistanov—"but you, leaving your lady, put mine on. . . ."

"What are you up to?" said Blistanov, frowning. "Coming here spreading scandal, is that it?"

"Oh, not at all! God forbid! You've misunderstood. . . . What am I here about? About boots! You did happen to be in room sixty-four, didn't you?"

"When?"

"Last night."

"Did you see me there?"

"No, I didn't see you." Mirkin sat down in confusion and hurriedly pulled off his boots. "I didn't see you but your lady flung your boots out to me. . . . Instead of my own, that is . . ."

"My dear sir, what right have you to make these scandalous assertions? I don't speak for myself but you're insulting a lady, and in the presence of her husband too!"

A terrible noise sounded in the theatre. King Bobesh, the outraged husband, suddenly went purple and struck the table with such force of fist that in the dressing room next door two actresses felt ill.

"Do you believe it?" Bluebeard shouted at him. "Do you believe this scoundrel? O . . . oh! If you want, I'll kill him like a dog? Want me to? I'll make mincemeat of him! I'll bash his head in!"

And all who walked that evening in the public garden by the summer theatre now relate they saw before the final act a barefoot man come fearful from the theatre down the central path with yellow face and eyes full of horror. In pursuit of him there ran a man in Bluebeard's costume with a revolver in his hand. No one saw what happened after that. It is only known that Mirkin, after meeting Blistanov, lay ill two weeks and to the words "I am a sick man. I suffer from rheumatism," began to add "I am disabled."

A Stage Manager under the Sofa
1885

(A Story from behind the Scenes)

DURING A QUICK-CHANGE vaudeville show Klavdia Matveyevna Dolskaya-Kauchukova, an artiste young and attractive and quite sublimely dedicated to the cause of art, ran into her dressing room and began to tear off her gypsy dress to slip on—in twinkling of an eye—a hussar's uniform. To avoid redundant creases and to slide the costume on as smooth and beautiful as possible, she thought, this dedicated artiste, that she'd strip off everything to the last thread and wear it over her body bare as Eve's.

And then, just after she was naked, crinkling in a little at the chill and sliding on the hussar's breeches, a sigh from someone sounded in her ear.

She stared wide-eyed and listened. Someone sighed again and seemed to whisper.

"Oh . . ! How heavy our sins . . ! Oh . . !"

Bewildered, she looked about and seeing nothing suspicious in her dressing room, decided to peep, just to be sure, under her only piece of furniture: the sofa. And what met her eye? There under the sofa: the long shape of a man.

"Who's there?" she shrieked, rebounding back in terror from the sofa and covering herself with the hussar's jacket.

"It's me . . ."—a trembling whisper came from under the sofa —". . . me. Don't be afraid! It's me! Sssssss!"

And in that snuffling whisper like a hissing frying pan she recognized quite clearly the voice of Indiukov, the stage manager.

"You?" she flared, red as a peony. "How . . . how dare you? You old devil, have you been there all this time? It's the limit."

"Dear old girl . . . Darling . . ." hissed Indiukov, poking his bald head out from under the sofa. "Don't be cross, sweetheart! Kill me, crush me like a snake, but don't make a noise. I saw nothing, I see nothing now, nor do I want to. No need to cover yourself, my darling, my splendid beauty. Listen to an old man, one foot already in his grave. Why I'm sprawling here is . . . just to save my life. I'm done for. Look, the hairs of my head are standing on end. The husband of my little Glashenka, Pryndin, has arrived from Moscow. He's marching up and down the theatre now, he's going to do for me. It's terrible! There's not only Glashenka, I owe him five thousand, the swine!"

"What's that to me? Get yourself out of here this minute or I . . . I don't know what I'll do to you, you devil!"

"Sssss! Darling, sssss! I'm begging on my knees, grovelling. Where am I to hide from him if not with you? Anywhere else he'll find me but he'll not dare come in here. Oh, I beg you! Oh, please! I saw him two hours ago. It was during the first act. I was standing in the wings and I saw him coming up on stage from the audience."

"You mean to say you've been crawling about here through the entire performance . . ."—she cried at him in horror—". . . and seen everything!"

The stage manager burst into tears.

"I'm trembling. I'm shaking, my darling, shaking! He'll kill me, the swine! He's shot at me once already . . . in Nizhni. . . . It was in the papers!"

"Oh . . . ! This has become intolerable. Get out. I have to dress and go on stage. Clear off or I'll scream, I'll have hysterics! I'll fling the lamp at you!"

"Sssss! You're my last hope . . . my lifebelt. Fifty roubles on your salary, only don't chase me out. Fifty!"

The actress clutched a little heap of clothing over herself and ran to the door to scream. Indiukov crawled after her on hands and knees and grabbed her leg above the ankle.

"Seventy-five roubles, only don't chase me out!" he hissed, choking. "And I'll add on half the benefit money!"

"You liar!"

"God be my witness! I swear it! So I'll be up the spout if I don't! Half the benefit money and seventy-five roubles on your pay!"

Dolskaya-Kauchukova quivered indecisive a moment and came away from the door.

"Go on, you're making it all up . . ." she said tearfully.

"May earth open and swallow me! Let me never see heaven! Am I that sort of scoundrel?"

"All right then," the actress agreed. "But don't you forget! And now then, creep back under the sofa."

Indiukov sighed deeply and crept puffing under the sofa and Dolskaya-Kauchukova quickly started to dress. She was ashamed and even scared to think a strange man lay under the sofa in her dressing room; but it so cheered her up to realise that she'd only given in for the sake of her sublime art that, some time later, as she flung off the hussar's uniform, not only was she cross no longer but she rather felt for him.

"You'll get yourself dirty there, dear Kuzma Alexeivitch! The things I put under that sofa!"

———

The vaudeville came to an end. They called her back eleven times and gave her a bouquet with ribbons on it inscribed: "Stay with us."

Going back to her dressing room after the ovation, she met Indiukov in the wings. Scruffy, filthy and dishevelled, the stage manager was beaming and rubbing his hands with delight.

"Ha ha! Just imagine, my darling!" he began, going up to her. "Have a laugh at this old fool! Imagine! It just wasn't Pryndin at all. To the devil with him, his long red beard put me all wrong! Pryndin has a long red beard as well. I made a mistake, stupid old idiot. I put you out for nothing, my lovely one!"

"Yes, but look here, don't forget what you promised me," said Dolskaya-Kauchukova.

"I'm not forgetting. I'm not forgetting, my dear, but, sweetheart, it wasn't Pryndin at all. Our agreement concerned Pryndin, so why should I keep to it, if it wasn't Pryndin? If it had been Pryndin, of course, it would be different, but, as you see, I made a mistake. I took some other funny bloke for Pryndin!"

"That's downright rotten!" the actress shouted angrily. "Rotten! A filthy trick!"

"Well, if it was Pryndin, of course, you'd have every right to insist I keep to the agreement, but the devil knows who he is. Maybe he's a cobbler or a tailor, say, do I still have to pay for him? I'm an honest man. I understand these things."

And he went off, still babbling and waving his arms.

"If it was Pryndin, then, of course, I'd be committed . . . but he's some unknown fellow . . . some chap with red hair . . . God knows who . . . but certainly not Pryndin."

Misery
1886

"To Whom Shall I Tell My Grief?"

DUSK. Big wet snow-flakes whirling around the just-lit lamps and settling on roof-tops, backs of horses, shoulders, caps.

Iona Potapov, sledgeman, is white all over like a ghost. Bent in on himself as far as living human body can be, he sits on the box, not moving at all. If all of a snowdrift fell over him, not even then, you think, would he feel need to shake it off.

His little mare is also white and still; with her stillness, her angular shape and her straight legs like sticks she has the look of a gingerbread horse sold for a penny. To all appearances she's sunk in thought. Any creature dragged from the plow, from familiar grey landscape and shoved down here, in this morass of monstrous lights, unceasing roar and rushing people, how can it help but brood . . . ?

Iona and his little mare have not stirred from that spot a long time now. They came out of the courtyard before dinner but no fares so far, no fares at all; and now the evening shadows are gathering over the town, the pale light of the lamps becomes more vivid, the street bustle noisier.

"Sledgeman, to Viborgskaya!" hears Iona. "Sledgeman!"

Iona starts, and through eyelashes plastered with snow sees a soldier in greatcoat and hood.

71

"To Viborgskaya!" repeats the soldier. "Are you asleep or what? To Viborgskaya!"

To show he is willing Iona clutches the reins, scattering cakes of snow from the mare's back and shoulders.

The soldier sits down in the sledge. The sledgeman clacks his lips, cranes his neck like a swan, rises a little and more from habit than need shakes his whip. The little mare too cranes her neck, crooks her stick-like legs and hesitantly sets off.

"Which way are you pushing, devil?" Iona hears immediate shouts from a dark mass shifting to and fro. 'Where the devil are you going? Keep to the r . . . right!"

"You don't know how to drive! Keep to the right!" shouts the soldier.

A coachman curses from his coach, a man crossing the road and bumping the mare's nose with his shoulder stares angrily and shakes snow from his sleeve. Iona fidgets on the box as on needles, sticks his elbows into his sides and moves his eyes like a madman as if not knowing where he is or why.

"Such scoundrels, all of them!" jokes the soldier. "Look how they just try to bump into you or fall under the horse's feet. They do it on purpose."

Iona looks at his passenger and moves his lips. He wants to say something, it seems, but only a hoarse noise comes from his throat.

"What?" asks the soldier.

Iona twists his mouth in a smile and croaks, straining his throat:

"Sir, my . . . my son died this week."

"H'm . . . What did he die of?"

"Who can know that? Must be of fever . . . Three days he was in hospital and died . . . God's will."

"Out of the way, devil!" comes out of the darkness. "Gone mad or what, old dog! Use your eyes!"

"Drive on, drive on . . ." says the passenger. "We won't get there till tomorrow at this rate. Get a move on, will you!"

Again the sledgeman cranes his neck, rises a little and swings the whip with clumsy grace. Several times he looks round at the passenger but he has shut his eyes, apparently in no mood to listen.

Putting his passenger down at Viborgskaya, Iona stops at a tavern, then sits again, huddled and quite still on the box. Again wet snow plasters him white, the little mare also. An hour passes; another . . .

Along the pavement come three young men stamping galoshes noisily and quarrelling together, two of them tall and thin, the other small and humpbacked.

"Sledgeman, to Police Bridge!" shouts the hunchback in cracked voice. "Three of us. . . . Twenty copecks!"

Iona tugs the reins and clacks his lips. Twenty copecks isn't fair rate but payment is no matter to him. A rouble or a five copeck piece, it's all the same to him now if only he has a passenger . . . The young men, pushing and swearing, come to the sledge and all three at once scramble up on the seat. A question faces them: which two will sit, which one stand? After long wrangling, bad temper and abuse they conclude that the hunchback must stand because he is smallest.

"Well then, drive on!" croaks the hunchback, settling into place and breathing down Iona's neck. "Whip away! Well, brother, what a cap you've got! You won't find a worse in all of Petersburg . . ."

"He he . . . He he . . ." laughs Iona. "It's such a one. . . ."

"Well then, you, 'Such a one!', drive on! Are you going to go all the way like this? Eh? Want it in the neck?"

"My head's splitting . . ." says one of the tall ones. "Yesterday at Dukmasov's, Vaska and I, we drank four bottles of brandy."

"I can't understand why you tell lies!" The other tall one gets angry. "Lying like a brute!"

"God strike me down! It's true. . . ."

"Well, if that's true, then a louse coughs!"

"He he . . ." giggles Iona. "Jo . . . jolly gentlemen!"

"Pah, the devil take you!" snaps the hunchback. "Will you

get going, you lump of cholera, or will you not? Is this the way you drive? Slash her with your whip! Oh, the devil, oh! Give her a lovely one!"

Iona feels behind his back the hunchback's fidgeting body and quivering voice. He hears swearing come at him, sees people, and little by little the feeling of loneliness lifts from his chest. The hunchback curses till he chokes on a fancy, treble-barreled oath and bursts out coughing. The tall ones start talking about a certain Nadezhda Petrovna. Iona glances back at them. Then he waits for a brief pause, glances back again and mutters:

"This week my . . . my . . . er . . . son died!"

"We're all going to die . . ." sighs the hunchback, wiping his lips after coughing. "Come on, drive on, drive on! Gentlemen, I just can't put up with crawling like this! When is he going to get us there?"

"Then give him something to cheer him up . . . in the neck!"

"Do you hear, you lump of cholera? I'll make your neck smart. Standing on ceremony with your sort, we might as well walk . . . Do you hear, Snake? Or don't you give a damn what we say?"

And Iona hears more than feels a slap on his neck.

"He he . . ." he laughs. "Jolly gentlemen . . . Your good health!"

"Sledgeman, are you married?" asks one tall one.

"Me, eh? He he . . . Jo . . . jolly gentlemen! The only wife for me these days . . . is the damp earth . . . He ho ho! . . . The grave I mean! . . . There's my son dead and I'm alive . . . Strange business, death mistook the door . . . Instead of coming for me it came for him . . ."

And Iona turns round to tell them how his son died but then the hunchback sighs softly and declares they are there at last, thank God. Iona takes his twenty copecks and stares a long time after the topers, who disappear into a dark doorway. Once more he is alone and once more there is silence for him. . . . Misery, calmed a brief time, comes back and tears his heart more cruelly. Anxiously, tormentedly, his eyes search restlessly the moving crowds on both sides of the street: can't he find a single one at least among these thousands who will listen to him? But the crowds rush by, heeding neither Iona nor his misery . . . Misery is huge, boundless. Let his heart break and misery flow out, then it would flood the whole world so it seems; and yet it is not seen. It is lodged in such an unimportant shell, you couldn't find it with a candle in the daylight . . .

Iona sees the house-porter with a parcel and decides to speak to him.

"Friend, what would the time be?" he asks.

"Ten or so. . . . Why've you stopped here, then? Move on."

Iona drives a few paces, cranes over and gives in to misery . . . To speak to people seems to him altogether useless. But not five minutes are gone before he sits up, shakes his head as if he feels sharp pain and tugs the reins . . . He can take no more.

"Back to the yard!" he decides. "Back to the yard!"

And the little mare, as if understanding his thought, begins to trot.

An hour and a half later Iona is sitting by a big dirty stove. On the stove, on the ground and on benches people lie snoring. The air is stuffy and oppressive. . . . Iona looks at the sleeping people, scratches himself and is sorry he came home so early . . .

"I've not made enough to pay for the oats," he thinks. "That's why misery's with me. A man who knows his job . . . who eats his fill and so does his horse, he's content all the time . . ."

In one of the corners a young coachman rises, grunts sleepily and reaches for the water-bucket.

"Felt like a drink?" Iona asks him.

"Seemed the way of it, yes!"

"Well, well . . . Good health . . . But my son, brother, he's dead . . . Did you hear? This week, in the hospital . . . What a business!"

Iona watches for the effect of his words but sees nothing. The young man has covered up his head and is asleep already. The old man sighs and scratches . . . As the young man thirsted for water, he thirsts to speak. It will be a week soon since his son died and he has spoken properly of it to no-one . . . He must speak about it plainly, deliberately . . . He must tell how his son fell ill, how he suffered, what he said before death came, how he died . . . He must describe the funeral and his visit to the hospital for his dead son's clothes . . . Anisia, his daughter, is still out in the country . . . He must talk about her too . . . Yes, all kinds of things he can talk about now. The one who listens ought to sigh, show sorrow and lament . . . Better still if he spoke to a woman. Yes, they're silly but they start weeping at a couple of words.

"I'll go out and have a look at the mare," thinks Iona. "You've always time to sleep . . . You can sleep, don't worry . . ."

He gets dressed and goes to the stable where the mare is. He thinks about oats, hay and the weather . . . As for his son, when he's alone, he can't think about him . . . To talk about him to someone, that's possible, but to think of him and picture to himself what he was like, it's unbearable anguish . . .

"Munching?" Iona asks his mare as he sees her shining eyes. "Go on, munch, munch . . . If we've not made enough for oats, we'll eat hay . . . Yes . . . I've gotten too old for driving now . . . My son should be driving, not me . . . He was a real sledgeman. . . . If only he were alive . . ."

Iona is silent a short time, then goes on:

"That's how it is, mate, my little mare . . . Kuzma Ionitch is gone . . . Departed this life . . . For no reason he went and died . . . Now let's say you had a little foal, and you were its own natural mother. . . . And all at once, let's say, this same foal departed this life. . . . Wouldn't you be sorry?"

The little mare munches, listens and breathes on her master's hands . . .

Iona is carried away and tells her the whole story . . .

Aniuta
1886

IN THE CHEAPEST room of a furnished boarding-house,
The Lisbon, a third-year medical student, Stepan Klotchkov,
was striding to and fro, determinedly swotting his anatomy. The
constant hard cramming made his mouth dry and brought sweat
out on his forehead.

Aniuta, the girl who lived with him, sat on a stool by the
window which was coated with a tracery of frost: she was a
little, thin brunette, twenty-five, very pale, with gentle grey
eyes. Leaning over, she was embroidering with red thread the
collar of a man's shirt, in a hurry to be finished . . .

The clock in the corridor struck dully two o'clock but still
the room had not been tidied. Blankets rumpled, pillows, books
and clothing scattered about, a big dirty basin full of soap suds
and floating cigarette ends, litter on the floor—it all seemed to
have been bundled into a pile, shuffled and rumpled together on
purpose . . .

"The right lung consists of three sections. . . ." repeated Klotchkov. "Divisions: Upper section at front wall of chest stretches
to the fourth or fifth rib, at the side to the fourth rib . . . and
behind to the *Spina scapulae*. . . ."

Striving to imagine what he had just read, Klotchkov looked
up at the ceiling. Not getting the picture clear, he began feeling
for his upper ribs through his vest.

"These ribs are like piano keys," he said. "To avoid mistakes
you just have to get used to them. You have to study them on

the skeleton and the living body . . . Oh, come on Aniuta, let me find where they are."

Aniuta left her sewing, took off her blouse and straightened up. Klotchkov sat down opposite her, frowned and began to count her ribs.

"H'm . . . You can't feel the first rib . . . It's behind the collar bone . . . This must be the second rib . . . That's it . . . Here's the third . . . Here's the fourth . . . H'm . . . That's it . . . What are you wriggling for?"

"Your fingers are cold."

"Now, now . . . You'll live. Don't writhe about. This is the third rib then and this is the fourth . . . You look so skinny but I can scarcely feel your ribs. This is the second . . . This is the third . . . No, it gets confusing, you can't make it clear . . . I'll have to draw it . . . Where's my charcoal crayon?"

Klotchkov took the crayon and traced some parallel lines on Aniuta's breast along the ribs.

"Jolly good! Plain as the palm of my hand . . . Well, now we can sound you . . . Stand up then!"

Aniuta stood up and lifted her chin. Klotchkov set about tapping her, becoming too engrossed to notice that her lips, nose and fingers were turning blue with cold. Aniuta shivered and was afraid the student, noticing, would stop marking her and tapping her and then, perhaps, do badly in the exam.

"Now it's all clear," said Klotchkov, ceasing to tap her. "You sit like that and don't rub off the marks and I'll do a bit more swotting."

And the student began to walk to and fro again, studying, while Aniuta, like a tattooed woman, with black stripes across her breast, sat shrivelling up with cold and thinking. She didn't usually speak much, was always quiet, thinking, thinking . . .

In all six or seven years of drifting from one bed-sitter to another she had known five other men like Klotchkov. They had all finished their courses now and gone out into the world and as respectable people had forgotten all about her long ago. One of them lived in Paris, two were doctors, a fourth an artist, and a fifth, they said, even a Professor by now. Klotchkov was

78

the sixth. Soon he would finish his studies like the others and go out into the world. The future would be fine for him, no doubt; very likely Klotchkov would be a big man one day; but things were really bad for him now: Klotchkov had no tobacco, no tea, and only four lumps of sugar left. She really must hurry up and finish her embroidery, take it to the woman who gave her the work and buy tea and tobacco with the twenty-five copecks.

"All right to come in?" said a voice at the door.

Aniuta quickly threw a woollen shawl over her shoulders. Fetisov, the painter, came in.

"I've come with a request to you," he began to Klotchkov, glaring out fiercely from under his long, dangling hair. "Do me a favour. Let me have your pretty little girl for an hour or two. I'm painting a picture, you see, and without a model it's quite impossible."

"Ah, with pleasure!" agreed Klotchkov. "Off you go, Aniuta."

"The things I've had to shut my eyes to there!" murmured Aniuta softly.

"Now then, that's enough! The man wants you for his art and not for any monkey tricks. Why not help him if you can?"

Aniuta began to get dressed.

"And what are you painting?" asked Klotchkov.

"Psyche. Splendid subject but all the same it's not working out: I'm painting with different models all the time. Yesterday I was painting one with blue legs. 'Why are your legs blue?' I asked her. 'It's my stockings,' she said. 'The colour comes off.' And you're still swotting. You're a lucky chap to be so patient."

"Medicine's the sort of job you can't get on with if you don't swot."

"H'm . . . Excuse me, Klotchkov, but you live like a pig, it's frightful! The devil knows the way you live!"

"Is that so? It's impossible to live any other way . . . I only get twelve roubles a month from my father and it's hard to live decently on that money."

"That may be . . ." said the painter, making a wry disdainful face, ". . . but all the same you could live better. An intelligent man ought to have taste. Isn't that so? But the devil knows how things go here! The bed not made, slops, mess . . . Yesterday's porridge still on the plates . . . Ugh!"

"That's true," said the student, becoming embarrassed, "but Aniuta hasn't had time to clear up today. She's been busy all along."

When the painter and Aniuta had gone, Klotchkov lay on the sofa and began to study lying down; then by chance he dropped off to sleep to wake again after an hour, prop up his head with his fists and brood gloomily. The painter's words came back to him, that an intelligent man ought certainly to have taste, and now his surroundings did indeed seem nauseating and repulsive. He foresaw, as through a window in his mind, his own future when he would receive patients in his surgery and take tea in a spacious dining-room, his wife there with him, a lady of quality; and now that basin with soap suds and floating cigarette ends looked unbelievably foul. And Aniuta herself appeared in his mind's eye, sloppy and to be pitied . . . And he decided to give her up at once, no matter what.

When she came back from the painter and took off her coat, he got up and spoke to her earnestly:

"Now then, my darling . . . Sit down and listen. We have to part. The fact is I don't want to live with you anymore."

Aniuta had come back from the painter tired out and ready to drop. Standing so long as a model had pinched in her features and her chin was sharper. She said nothing in reply to his words, only her lips began to tremble.

"You agree that sooner or later anyhow we'd have to part," said the student. "You're nice and kind and you're not stupid, you'll understand. . . ."

Aniuta put her coat on again, silently wrapped her embroidery in paper and gathered up her needles and thread; she found the slip of paper with the four lumps of sugar and put it on the table by the book.

"This is your . . . sugar . . ." she said quietly and turned away to hide her tears.

"Now what are you crying for?" asked Klotchkov.

He walked around the room ill at ease and said: "You're a strange girl and that's a fact. . . . You know yourself, don't you, we shall have to part. We can't be together for ages."

She had already gathered up all her things and already turned to him to say goodbye and he felt sorry for her.

"Let her stay for another week, shall I?" he wondered. "Well, let her stay on at any rate, and at the end of a week I'll tell her to go."

And, angry at his own weak will, he shouted at her gruffly:

"Why are you standing there, then? Go if you're going, but if you don't want to, take off your coat and stay! Stay!"

Aniuta took off her coat, silently, with stealth, then blew her nose, also with stealth, sighed and without a sound went back to her habitual place—the stool by the window.

The student snatched up his textbook and again walked to and fro.

"The right lung consists of three sections . . ." he repeated. "Upper section at front wall of chest stretches to the fourth or fifth rib. . . ."

And somebody in the corridor shouted at the top of his voice:

"Grigorey, the samovar!"

The Witch
1886

NIGHT COMING ON. Saveli Gikin, the sexton, lay in a huge bed at his lodge by the church, not yet asleep although it was his habit always to drop off at the same time as his hens. At one end of a greasy patchwork quilt of many-coloured rags his coarse red hair peeped out while from the other stuck big feet, long unwashed. He was listening . . .

His lodge was set into the wall around the church, one single window looking out to the open fields, where now a downright war was going on. It was hard to make out who was doing whom to death and for whose ruin such a tumult came in nature; but to judge from the never-ending evil roar, someone was getting it hot and strong. A sort of conquering power was hounding someone through the fields, roaring in the wood and on the church roof, thumping viciously on the window, raging and rending, while some defeated thing was wailing. Mournful weeping came now at the window, now on the roof, now in the stove: no cry for help therein, only misery, awareness all was too late, no hope of salvation.

The snowdrifts had a thin icy crust and on the trees tears trembled; while along highways and tracks flowed dark slushes of mud and melting snow. The thaw, in fact, was on the land but heaven could not see it through dark night and fiercely flung fresh snowflakes on the melting earth. And the wind floundered like a drunken man, not letting snow lie on the land but whirling it in darkness at its whim.

Saveli listened to the racket and frowned. The fact was that he knew or guessed at any rate what all this pother through the window was about and whose hand was behind it.

"I know . . . ," he muttered, waggling his finger accusingly under the quilt. "I know all about it."

On a stool at the window sat Raissa Nilovna, the sexton's wife. A little tin lamp on another stool, as if timid and distrusting its own power, cast dim flickering light on her broad shoulders, the lovely tempting lines of her body and her thick plait reaching down to the floor. She was making sacks out of coarse hemp. Her hands moved nimbly but all her body, the glimmer of her eyes, her brows, plump lips and white neck were quite still, absorbed in monotonous, mechanical work, seeming asleep. Just occasionally she lifted her head to rest her tired neck, glanced a moment at the window beyond which the snowstorm roared, then stooped again over the sacking. No desire, no grief, no joy— her beautiful face, snub-nosed and dimple-cheeked, expressed nothing at all: just as a beautiful fountain expresses nothing when it does not play.

But now she finished a sack, threw it aside and, stretching sensuously, looked steadily at the window with lack-lustre eyes. Drops like tears ran down the panes, whitened by short-lived snowflakes which, falling on the glass, glanced at Raissa and melted . . .

"Come and lie down!" muttered the sexton.

His wife stayed silent. But suddenly her lashes flickered and an intent gleam came in her eyes. Saveli, watching the look on her face continuously from under the quilt, stuck out his head and asked:

"What is it?"

"Nothing . . . Looks as if somebody's coming . . ." she quietly replied.

The sexton thrust off the quilt with arms and legs, knelt up on the bed and looked dull-eyed at his wife. The timid light lit his hairy, pock-marked face and flowed over his coarse, tousled hair.

"Do you hear?" asked his wife.

Through the storm's monotonous howling he caught a scarcely-heard, thin jingling drone like a gnat's whine, angry when you stop it settling on your cheek.

"It's the post . . ." muttered Saveli, sitting on his heels.

The route the post took was three versts from the church. In gusty weather, with the wind blowing from the highroad towards the church, they could hear the bells from the lodge.

"God, chasing about in weather like this!" murmured Raissa.

"It's government work. Want or not, you've got to go . . ."

The drone hovered in the air and died away.

"It's gone past!" said Saveli, lying down.

But he hadn't time to cover himself up in the quilt before the clear peal of a little bell reached his ears. The sexton glared uneasily at his wife, jumped off the bed and waddled up and down alongside the stove. The bell sounded a little longer then died away again as if cut short.

"Don't hear it . . ." mumbled the sexton, stopping and screwing up his eyes at his wife.

But there and then the wind beat on the window, blowing with it the thin, jingling drone . . . Saveli went pale, grunted and flopped bare-footed along the floor again.

"The postman's in a whirlwind!" he wheezed, scowling spitefully at his wife. "Do you hear? The postman's in a whirlwind! . . . I know . . . Think I don't understand the lot?" he muttered. "I know all about it, devil take you!"

"What is it you know?" asked his wife quietly, not taking her eyes from the window.

"I know this: that it's all your doing, she-devil! All your doing, may you be damned for it! The snowstorm and the postman in a whirlwind. It's you who've caused it! You!"

"You're raving, stupid . . ." said his wife quietly.

"I've been on your track a long time and can see. Just when we got married, the first day even, I saw you'd blood of a bitch!"

"Pah!" gasped Raissa, heaving her shoulders and crossing herself. "Cross yourself, idiot!"

"A witch is a witch, that's what she is!" went on Saveli in

hollow whining tone, hurriedly blowing his nose on his shirt hem. "And though you're my wife, and though you're from a religious family, I'll tell about you even at confession, say what you are . . . Won't I just? Protect me, God, for pity's sake! Last year on the eve of Daniel the Prophet and his Three Companions there was a snowstorm—and what then? The overseer came in here to warm himself. Then on St. Alexei's day the ice broke on the river, and it brought the village constable . . . All night here with you he was, tattling, cursed brute, and in the morning when he came out I looked at him, so I did, and saw he had rings under his eyes and all his cheeks sunken in! What about that? In Lent there were two storms and both times a hunter came and stayed the night. I saw the whole thing, may he be damned for it! The whole thing! Oh, blushing redder than a crab you are! Aha!"

"You didn't see a thing . . ."

"Oh yes I did! And this winter, before Christmas, the day of the Ten Cretian Martyrs, when the snowstorm went on all day and night . . . remember . . . the clerk of the Marshal lost his way and turned up here, the dog! And what a man to let tempt you! Pah, a clerk! Worth setting God's weather seething for! Snotty-nosed driveller, crawling so low you can't even see him, spots all over his snout and neck lop-sided . . . Might not be so bad if he were good-looking but *him* . . . Pah! Ugly as the devil!"

The sexton breathed in, wiped his lips and listened. He couldn't hear the bell but then the wind struck the roof and its drone came again from the dark beyond the window.

"And now it's the same!" went on the sexton. "Not for nothing the postman's in a whirlwind! Damn my eyes if the postman isn't coming after you! Oh, the devil knows what he's about, a ready helper he is! He's whirling him, whirling him and leading him here. I know . . . I have eyes . . . You can't hide yourself, you're Satan's plaything, lust of the devil! As soon as the snowstorm started, I saw into your mind."

"Idiot that you are!" His wife smiled. "Why, then, in that stupid head of yours, do you think I make the storm?"

"Gah! Grin then! Whether it's you or not, I know this: when

the blood begins to tingle in you, there's a storm, and when there's a storm, it brings some madman here. That's the way it goes every time! It must be you!"

For greater effect the sexton laid his finger on his forehead, closed his left eye and murmured sing-song:

"Oh, the folly of it! The curse of Judas! If you are a human being, really, and not a witch, you should think this in your head: what if he's not an overseer, not a hunter, not a clerk, but the devil in that shape? Eh? That's what you should think!"

"Oh, it's stupid that you are, Saveli!" sighed his wife, looking at him with pity. "When my Dad was alive and we lived here all sorts of people came to him to be cured of the fever: from the village and the settlements and the Armenian farms. Look, they came every day and no one called them devils. But if somebody comes once a year to us, to get warm again when there's a storm, you start wondering, you idiot, and there and then get all sorts of ideas."

The logic of what she said affected Saveli. He set his bare legs wide apart, stooped his head, and thought about it. He was still not firmly convinced of his suspicions and his wife's sincere, unworried tone bewildered him: yet all the same after a little thought he shook his head and said:

"It's not as if they're old men or cripples, it's all young men who are after spending the night. . . . Why is that? If they only wanted to get warm, all right, but it's mischief they're after. No, woman, in all this world no creatures are more cunning than the female kind! Proper brains in you lot? No, my God, less than a starling has, but the devil's own cunning . . . O . . . oh, protect us, Queen of Heaven! . . . There it is, the postman's bell! As soon as the snowstorm started I saw all that was in your mind! Witchcraft, you spider!"

"Oh, why do you stick onto me so, you curse!" His wife lost patience. "Why do you stick onto me, like tar?"

"Well I do it because if this night, God forbid, anything happens . . . you hear . . . if anything happens, then tomorrow as soon as it's light I'll go to Father Nikodim and tell him everything. 'Father Nikodim,' I'll say, 'I beg your gracious pardon, but she is a witch. Why is she a witch? H'm? You want to know why? Very well then . . . Here's the whole story.' And woe betide you, woman! Not only on the dreadful Day of Judgement but here on earth, alive, you'll be punished. Not for nothing are prayers set down in the book against your kind!"

Suddenly at the window there was a knock, so loud and strange that Saveli went pale and cowered in fear. His wife started up and also went pale.

"For God's sake let us in to get warm," came a thick quivering voice. "Who's there? Do us a kindness! We've been driven from our way."

"But who are you?" asked Raissa, afraid to look towards the window.

"Post!" answered a second voice.

"Your witchcraft's worked then!" Saveli flapped his hand. "That's what it is! I'm right! . . . Well, watch out for me!"

The sexton took two leaps to the bed, flung himself on the feather mattress and with angry snort turned his face to the wall. Soon a cold draught blew on his back. The door creaked and a tall male figure caked from head to foot with snow appeared on the threshold. Behind him glimmered another, just as white.

"And do I bring the bags in?" asked the second in a hoarse low voice.

"Well, we can't leave them there!"

As he spoke, the first one began untying his hood but couldn't wait and pulled it off with his cap and flung it spitefully towards the stove. Then, dragging off his coat, he chucked it in the same place and without a word of greeting began walking up and down.

He was a young, fair-haired postman in worn-out uniform and grimy, rust-coloured boots. Warmed by his walking he sat down at the table, stretching his muddy feet out to the sacks and propping his chin with his fists. His pale face, blotched with red, bore traces still of recent pain and fear. Distorted in anger, marks of anguish, physical and moral, still fresh on it, melting snow in brows, moustache and curving beard, it was a handsome face.

"A dog's life like this!" the postman muttered, looking round the walls as if not believing he was in the warmth.

"We were nearly done for. If it wasn't for your light, I don't know how things would have gone. . . . Devil only knows when all this lot will be over! This dog's life never ends!

"Where is it we've got to?" he asked, lowering his voice and glancing up at the sexton's wife.

"Guliaevski Hill on General Kalinovski's estate," she answered, startled and blushing.

"Hear that, Stepan?" The postman turned to the driver, wedged in the doorway, a huge leather bag on his back. "We've got to Guliaevski Hill."

"Yes . . . Long way out!"

Spluttering out the words in a wheezy sigh, the driver went away and a little later brought back another smaller bag, then went out yet again and this time brought with him the postman's sword on its broad belt, long and flat shaped like the one they carve in cheap woodcuts for Judith at the bed of Holofernes. He laid the bags along the wall and went into the passage, sat down there and lit his pipe.

"Perhaps you'd like some tea after your journey?" asked Raissa.

"What's the point of drinking tea here?" The postman frowned. "We've got to get warm quick and go or we'll be late for the mail train. We'll stay ten minutes then be off. Only please help and show us the way . . ."

"It's God's own weather this, to punish us!" sighed Raissa.

"H'm. That's so . . . And who might you be in this place?"

"Us? We live here, by the church. . . . We belong to the clergy. That's my husband, lying there. Saveli, get up and say good evening. Once this used to be a parish of its own but eighteen months ago they did away with it. In those days, of course, there were gentry here and other people, church services were needed. But now, with the gentry gone, you can see for yourself there isn't a living for the clergy, the nearest village is Markovka and it's five versts away. So Saveli has lost his place . . . and now he's the watchman. He has to look after the church . . ."

And there and then she let the postman understand that, if

Saveli would see the General's wife and ask her for a letter to
His Grace the Bishop, they would give him a better living; but
he wouldn't because he was lazy and afraid of people.

"All the same we belong to the clergy . . ." added Raissa.

"But what do you live on?" asked the postman.

"There's a meadow and a kitchen garden that belong to the
church. But we only get a little from them." Raissa sighed. "Father Nikodim, the deacon, old greedy eyes, preaches here on
St. Nicolas Day in the summer, yes, and on the winter one as
well, and for that takes practically the lot himself. Nobody sticks
up for us!"

"Liar!" snorted Saveli. "Father Nikodim is a saintly soul, a
light of the church, and if he takes it, that's his right!"

"You've a grumpy one there!" The postman grinned, "Have
you been married long?"

"Since the last Sunday in Lent three years ago. In the old
days my father lived here as sexton and then, when the time
came for him to die, he went to the Consistory and so that I
could have a place here still, he asked for some unmarried sexton
to be sent here and to be my husband. And I married him."

"Aha, so you killed two birds with one stone!" said the postman, looking at Saveli's back. "You got a job and took a wife."

Saveli jerked his leg impatiently and moved nearer to the
wall. The postman left the table, stretched himself and sat down
on a mail bag. He thought a moment, then rumpled the bag with
his hands, shifted his sword the other side of him and sprawled,
one foot dangling out to the floor.

"A dog's life . . ." he muttered, putting his hands under his
head and closing his eyes. "Even on a wild Tartar I wouldn't
wish a life like this."

Soon there was quiet. The only sounds were Saveli sniffing
and the postman breathing slow and even, bringing out with
every breath a deep and lingering "h . . h . . h . ." From time to
time there was a noise in his throat like a little creaking wheel
and his leg jerked and rustled against the bag.

Saveli turned himself under the quilt and looked slowly about.

His wife was sitting on the stool, pressing her palms against her cheeks and gazing at the postman, her stare quite fixed, like that of one surprised and frightened.

"Well, what are you gaping at?" whispered Saveli angrily.

"What's it to you? Lie down!" replied his wife, not taking her eyes from the fair-haired head.

Saveli blew fiercely all the breath from his chest and turned back sharply to the wall. Three minutes later he turned round restlessly again, knelt up in bed and setting his hands against the pillow, squinted at his wife. She was still as ever, staring at their guest, her cheeks pale and her glance shining with strange fire. The sexton grunted, crawled on his belly off the bed and, reaching the postman, covered his face with a handkerchief.

"Why'd you do that?" asked his wife.

"So that the light doesn't strike his eyes."

"Then put the light out altogether!"

Saveli glanced suspiciously at his wife, thrust out his lips to the lamp but then at once thought better of it and clasped his hands.

"Well, isn't that the cunning of the devil?" he cried. "Eh? Well, is there a creature more cunning than womankind?"

"Ah, you devil in a cassock!" hissed his wife, wrinkling up her face in anger. "Just you wait!"

And settling more comfortably, she stared again at the postman.

It didn't matter that his face was covered. His face took her attention less than the novelty of this man, all of him together. His chest was broad, powerful, his hands graceful and slender and his shapely, muscular legs were lovelier, more masculine by far than Saveli's two little stumps.

"Devil in a cassock I may be," said Saveli after a short pause, "but they've no business sleeping here. . . . Oh no. . . . Theirs is government work. We shall have to answer for keeping them here. If you take mail, then take it you do, you've no business sleeping."

"Eh, you!" he shouted into the passage. "You, driver . . .

what's your name? Shall I show you the way or what? Get up, no business sleeping when you're with the mail!"

And quite out of temper Saveli rushed to the postman and tugged him by the sleeve.

"Hey, sir! If you're going, well go. If you're not . . . it won't do. It's not right sleeping here."

The postman reared up, sat down, looked dull-eyed round the room and lay back again.

"But when are you going?" Saveli babbled on, tugging him by the sleeve. "That's what the post's about, getting there in good time, do you hear? I'll take you."

The postman opened his eyes. Warm and weary out of sweet first sleep, still not altogether awake, he saw, as in mist, Raissa's white neck and quite still, liquid gaze and closed his eyes and smiled as if all happened in dream.

"Come, how can you travel in such weather!" He heard a soft, woman's voice. "Better sleep, yes, sleep and it will do you good!"

"But the post?" muttered Saveli anxiously. "Who's going to take the post, then? Are you taking it? You?"

The postman opened his eyes again, and, glancing at dimples moving on Raissa's face, remembered where he was and understood what Saveli was saying. The thought of having to drive through cold darkness sent cold shudders running from his head to all his body and he huddled himself up.

"I might sleep another five minutes." He yawned. "I'll be late anyhow."

"But we might just get there in time," came a voice from the passage. "Look, times vary. With luck the mail train might be late."

The postman got up and, stretching luxuriously, began to put on his coat.

Saveli, seeing their guests prepare to go, actually neighed with delight.

"Help me, will you!" shouted the driver to him, lifting a mail bag from the floor.

The sexton rushed out to him and helped him drag the bags into the yard. The postman started to untangle a knot in his hood. And Raissa stared into his eyes as if intent to find a way there to his heart.

"You should have a drink of tea . . ." she said.

"I wouldn't refuse . . . but see, they're getting ready," he conceded. "As it was, we were late."

"Do stay!" she whispered, lowering her eyes and touching him at the sleeve.

The postman untangled the knot at last and, hesitant, flung the hood over his elbow. He felt warm standing close to Raissa.

"What a fine . . . neck you have . . ."

And he touched her neck with two fingers. Seeing she did not resist, he stroked with his hand her neck, her shoulder . . .

"Oh, how fine . . .

"Better stay . . . Better have a drink of tea. . . ."

"Where are you putting it? Butterfingers!" came the driver's voice from the yard. "Put it crossways."

"Better stay. . . . Listen how the wind howls!"

And still not altogether waking, unable yet to shake from him the spell of young and weary sleep, the postman suddenly was in the power of desire for whose sake postbags, mail trains—all things in this world—are quite forgotten. Fearfully, as if longing to run away or hide, he glanced at the door, seized Raissa by the waist and was just bending to put out the lamp when footsteps sounded in the passage and the driver appeared at the door. . . . Over his shoulder Saveli was peeping. The postman quickly dropped his arms and stood as if irresolute.

"All ready!" said the driver.

The postman stood a moment longer, lifted his head sharply as if waking at last and went out after the driver. Raissa was left alone.

"Well then, get in, show us the way!" she heard.

A single bell rang sluggishly, then another, and a long, clinking chain of sounds scudded away from the lodge.

When they had gradually faded, Raissa gave a start and nervously strode up and down. She was pale at first then blushed all over. Face twisted with hate, breath quivering, eyes shining with savage fury, she was like a pacing tigress in a cage, tormented by a red-hot iron. She stopped a moment and stared at where she lived. The bed filled nearly half the room, lay all along one wall, made up of filthy feather mattress, coarse grey pillows, quilt and rags of various sorts without a name. A shapeless ugly mess, this bed, almost like that which bristled always on Saveli's head when he bethought to oil his hair. Between the bed and the door to the passage loomed the dark stove with pots on it and hanging clouts. Everything, and Saveli too who had just gone from the place, was filthy, greasy, grimy as could be, so it was strange to see there the white neck of a woman and her fair dainty skin.

Raissa rushed to the bed, stretched out her hands as if longing to scatter, stamp and tear it all to bits, but then, as if afraid to touch the filth, recoiled and started pacing once again.

When, two hours later, Saveli came back, weary and plastered with snow, she lay already undressed in bed. Her eyes were shut but by the tremor that flickered on her face he guessed she wasn't asleep. On the way home he had promised himself to be quiet and not touch her till tomorrow yet once here he could not help but wound.

"You tried your witch's tricks for nothing: he's gone!" he said, grinning spitefully.

She was silent, only her chin flinched. Saveli slowly took off his clothes, crawled over his wife and lay by the wall.

"And tomorrow I'll tell Father Nikodim the kind of wife you are!" he muttered, curling himself up.

Raissa swiftly turned her face towards him and flashed her eyes.

"This place is alright for you," she said, "but go find yourself a wife in the forest. What kind of a wife am I for you? Curses on you! This burden stuck all the time round my neck, a lazybones, God forgive me!"

"Now, now, go to sleep!"

"How miserable I am!" she sobbed. "If you didn't exist, maybe I'd have married a merchant or some gentleman. If you didn't exist, I'd love my husband now! But the snow hasn't buried you, you haven't frozen out there on the highway!"

Raissa wept a long time. Then at last she gave a deep sigh and was quiet. The blizzard raged still beyond the window. In the stove, in the pipe, all round the outside walls something was wailing and Saveli felt it wailed within himself and in his own ears. He was sure at last, this evening, of his suspicions about his wife. That she had power, with the devil's help, over the winds and post horses he had no doubt. But to his greater grief this mystery, this supernatural savage power gave the woman lying by his side peculiar fascination not to be believed and never felt before. Because in folly, not knowing what he did, he cast a glamour over her, she became, so it seemed, whiter, smoother, more impenetrable. . . .

"Witch!" he snarled. "Pah! Hideous creature!"

All the same he waited till she was quiet and breathing easily then touched the back of her head with his fingers . . . held her thick plait in his hand. She did not feel it. . . . Then he became bolder and stroked her neck.

"Stop it!" she shouted and rapped him so hard on the nose with her elbow that sparks flickered in his eyes.

The pain in his nose faded quickly yet all his torment remained.

Love Affair with a Double-Bass
1886

SMICHKOV, THE MUSICIAN, was on his way from town to
Prince Bibulov's *dacha*, where, to celebrate a betrothal, an
evening of music and dancing was to take place. His huge double-
bass encased in leather on his back, he walked beside a river
where the cool waters flowed along, if not sublimely, then at least
with a certain lyricism.

"Why not take a dip?" he thought.

And without much further thinking he stripped and launched
his body into the cool stream.

It was a magnificent evening and Smichkov's poetic nature
began to be in harmony with his surroundings. But then a most
sweet feeling entranced his spirits; for, having swum along a
hundred paces, he saw a very lovely girl sitting on the steep
bank, fishing. He held his breath, struck quite still, a prey to
changing emotions: childhood memories, yearning for the past,
a stirring of love.

But, oh God, he thought he was able to love no longer! Since
he lost faith in humanity (when his darling wife ran off with
Sabarkin, the bassoon player, his friend) his heart was filled with
a sense of emptiness and he had become a misanthropist.

"What kind of life is this?" he'd asked himself more than once.
"What are we living for? Life is a myth, a day-dream . . . a
puppet show. . . ."

But now at the feet of this sleeping beauty (it was easy to
see she was asleep) he suddenly felt, despite his will, a thing in

95

his heart akin to love. He stayed a long time before her, feasting his eyes. . . .

"But that's enough . . ." he thought, breathing a deep sigh. "Farewell, lovely vision! It's time now for me to go to His Highness' ball. . . ."

And with yet another glance at the lovely girl he was starting to swim back when an idea flashed across his mind.

"I must leave her a thing to remember me by!" he thought. "I'll hitch something to her line. It will be a surprise from "an unknown stranger."

Smichkov swam quietly to the bank, gathered a bunch of field and water flowers, bound them with a stalk of goose foot and hitched them to the line.

The bunch sank down and with it took the pretty float.

Prudence, the natural order of things and the social position of my hero require that my love story should end just here. But, alas, the fate of an author is relentless. In clear despite of him his story will not end with the bunch of flowers. Against all sober sense and natural law the poor and humble double-bass player had to play a role of great importance in the life of a noble, rich and lovely young lady.

When he reached the bank, Smichkov was horrified: he couldn't see his clothes, someone had stolen them! While he'd been gazing lovingly upon the lovely girl, some unknown villains had made off with everything, except his double-bass and his top hat.

"Curses on you, breed of snakes!" he shouted. "It's not only the loss of clothes that makes my blood boil (for clothes wear out) but the thought that I must go stark naked and offend the laws of decency."

He sat down on his double-bass case and tried to seek a way out of his terrible dilemma.

"I can't walk naked to Prince Bibulov's!" he thought. "There'll be ladies! And what's more the thieves stole my rosin when they made off with my trousers."

He thought and thought in anguish till his temples hurt.

"Ah!" At last he remembered. "Not far from the bank in the bushes there's a footbridge. Till darkness comes I can sit under that bridge and then in the dusk of evening I'll sneak to the nearest peasant's hut."

Having thought the matter over, Smichkov put on his top hat, heaved up his double-bass behind him and trudged towards the bushes. Naked, his instrument on his back, he was like some mythical demigod of the ancient world.

And there, my reader, while my hero sits under the bridge and gives in to grief, we'll leave him for a while and return to the girl who was fishing. What happened to her? When she woke up and could not see her float on the water, she hurriedly tugged at the line. It tautened but neither float nor hook came up. Apparently Smichkov's bunch of flowers had become sodden and heavy in the water.

"Either a big fish is biting," she thought, "or else the hook is caught."

She tugged away at the line for a while and decided that the hook was caught.

"What a pity!" she thought. "In the evening when the fish bite so well! What shall I do?"

And without much thought the eccentric girl threw off her flimsy garments and submerged her lovely body to the marble shoulders in the stream. It wasn't easy to free the hook from the entangling bunch of flowers but work and patience won the day. After some fifteen minutes the lovely girl came radiant and happy out of the water, clutching the hook.

But an evil fate awaited her. The rogues who had stolen Smichkov's clothes, had snatched hers too, leaving only a jar of worms.

"Whatever shall I do now?" She burst into tears. "Can I possibly go about looking like this? No, never! I'd rather die! I'll wait till dusk, then go in the dark to my old nanny Agatha's and send her home for clothes. And in the meantime I'll go and hide under the footbridge."

97

My heroine, choosing the deepest grass and bending low, ran to the bridge. Creeping under it, she saw a naked man with musician's curls and hairy chest, screamed and lost her senses.

Smichkov was frightened too. At first he took her for a water nymph.

"Is this a mermaid come to lure me?" he wondered and the idea appealed for he had always had a high opinion of his looks. "If she's not a mermaid but a human being, then how do you explain that strange appearance? Why is she here under the bridge? And what's the matter with her?"

While he was considering these questions, the lovely girl came round.

"Don't kill me!" she murmured. "I'm Princess Bibulova. I implore you! You'll get a big reward! Just now I was untangling my hook in the water and some thieves stole away my new dress, my boots and everything!"

"Madam," said Smichkov in a pleading voice, "they stole my clothes as well. What's more they even took away the rosin that was in my trousers."

Double-bass players and trombonists are usually at a loss in crises: but Smichkov was a pleasant exception.

"Madam," he said after a little pause, "I see that my appearance embarrasses you. But you'll agree I can't go off in this state, any more than you can. Here's what I suggest: would you like to lie down in my double-bass case and cover yourself with the lid? That will hide you from me. . . ."

With these words Smichkov heaved his double-bass out of the case. For a moment it seemed a profanation of his sublime art to give up his case but his hesitation was short. The lovely girl lay down inside the case and curled up and Smichkov fastened the straps, feeling delighted that nature had given him such intelligence.

"Now, Madam, you cannot see me," he said. "Lie there and be at ease. When darkness comes, I'll carry you to your father's house. And then I can come back here for my double-bass."

When it was dusk Smichkov hoisted the case with the lovely girl on his shoulder and set off for Bibulov's *dacha*. His plan was this: he would go first to the nearest cottage, get some clothes there and then go on. . . .

"Every cloud's a silver lining . . ." he reflected, stirring up the dust with his bare feet and bending under his load. "For the warm sympathy I've shown his daughter in her plight, Bibulov is sure to reward me handsomely."

"Are you quite comfortable, Madam?" he asked in the tone of a *cavalier galant* requesting her to dance a quadrille. "I beg you, do not stand on ceremony and make yourself quite at home in my case!"

Suddenly it seemed to the gallant Smichkov that before him, shrouded in darkness, two human shapes were moving. Peering more closely, he was sure it wasn't an optical illusion: the shapes were certainly moving and what's more were carrying some sort of bundles. . . .

"Isn't that the thieves?" flashed into his mind. "They're carrying something. It's probably our clothes!"

Smichkov lowered his double-bass beside the path and dashed after the figures.

"Stop!" he shouted. "Stop! Seize them!"

The shapes looked round and seeing they were pursued took to their heels. The Princess heard running footsteps for a time and cries of "Stop!" Then all was still.

Smichkov kept up the chase, and very probably the lovely girl would have lain a long time in a field by the path but for a happy chance. It turned out that two of Smichkov's colleagues, Zhuchkov, the flutist, and Razmahaikin, the clarinetist, were passing at that time along that way to Bibulov's *dacha*. Stumbling upon the case, they stared at each other in surprise and flung up their arms.

"A double-bass!" said Zhuchkov. "But that's our Smichkov's double-bass. But how did it get here?"

"Something has probably happened to Smichkov," Razmahaikin decided. "Either he's drunk or he's been robbed. We'll take it with us."

Zhuchkov hoisted the case on his back and the musicians went on their way.

"What a devil of a weight!" the flutist kept grumbling all the way. "I wouldn't play this lumbering thing for anything in the world! Oh!"

Once they reached Prince Bibulov's *dacha* they put the case in the place reserved for the orchestra and went off to the buffet.

The chandeliers were just being lit. The fiancé Lakeitch, a counsellor at court and an official in the Highways Department, a very pleasant, handsome fellow, was standing in the middle of the ballroom, hands in pockets, chatting about music to Count Shkalikov.

"You know, Count," he said, "I came across a string player in Naples who worked perfect wonders. You don't believe me? On a double-bass, a common or garden double-bass, he produced such devilish trills it made you shiver. He played Strauss waltzes."

"Surely it's impossible . . ." said the Count with doubt in his voice.

"But I assure you. He even performed a Rhapsody of Liszt. I used to share a room with him and once, to pass the time, I learned from him how to play a Liszt Rhapsody on the double-bass."

"A Liszt rhapsody. . . . Hmmmm! You're joking. . . ."

"You don't believe me?" laughed Lakeitch. "Very well, I'll prove it to you. Let's go over to the orchestra."

The fiancé and the count went over to the orchestra, found the double-bass, started hurriedly to undo the straps . . . and oh, horror!

And now, as the reader, giving full rein to imagination, pictures the outcome of this musical controversy, let us return to Smichkov. . . . The poor musician, not having caught the thieves, returned to the spot where he put down his case but did not see his precious burden. Bewildered, he wandered back and forth along the path a few times and, still not finding it, decided he had come to the wrong path. . . .

"It's terrible!" he thought, plucking his hair and going freezing cold. "She'll suffocate in that case. I'm a murderer."

Till midnight he paced up and down the path, searching for his case, but in the end, exhausted, he set off for the footbridge.

"I'll search again at dawn," he decided.

But searching in the dawn brought just the same result and Smichkov decided to wait for nightfall under the bridge.

"I'll find her!" he muttered, taking off his top hat and clutching his hair. "Even if I search a year, I'll find her."

And still today the peasants living in the place relate that in the night time a sort of naked man is to be seen, overgrown with hair and in a top hat. From under the bridge sometimes you can hear the wheezing of a double-bass.

The Trick
1886

A clear winter noon . . .

A frost, hard and crackling, and Nadenka, holding me under the arm, had silver rime on curls at her temples and the down of her upper lip. We stood on a high hill and from our feet a slope, reflecting the sun like a mirror, stretched all the way down. Beside us was a little sledge upholstered in bright red cloth.

"Let's slide down, Nadejda Petrovna," I pleaded. "Just once. I assure you, we'll come through safe and sound."

But Nadenka was afraid. All the way down from her tiny galoshes to the bottom of the icy slope seemed a terrifying abyss, immeasurably deep. Her heart sank and her breathing stopped when she looked down or when I merely suggested sitting in the sledge. If she took a risk and hurtled into the abyss, what then? She'd die, lose her senses.

"I beg you," I said. "There's no need to be afraid. That's mean-spirited, you know, cowardice!"

At last Nadenka gave in and I saw from her face that she did it with fear for her life. I seated her, pale and trembling, in the sledge, clutched her hand and down we sped together into the abyss.

The sledge flew like a bullet. The cleaving air whipped, howling, into our faces, whistled in our ears, tore and tweaked at us in hurtful spite and tried to rive the heads from our shoulders. The wind's force took away our power to breathe. It was as if the devil himself had clutched us in his claws and with a roar was rushing us to hell. Everything about us blurred together in a single, headlong-rushing strip. Only a moment more, it seemed, and we would perish!

"I love you, Nadia!" I whispered.

The sledge began to move more quietly, more quietly, the roar of wind and the whirr of runners less fierce, we were free to breathe again and there we were, at last, at the bottom. Nadenka seemed neither alive nor dead. She was white, scarcely breathing. . . . I helped her up.

"I'll not go again for anything," she said, looking at me with wide eyes full of horror. "Not for anything on earth! I nearly died!"

After a little time she recovered and looked inquiringly into my eyes: had I said those four words or did she only seem to hear them in the wind? And I stood beside her, smoking, and carefully examining my glove.

She took me by the arm and for a long time we walked about the hill. Clearly the puzzling question gave her no peace. Were those words spoken or weren't they? Yes or no? Yes or no? It was a matter of pride, of honour, of life and happiness, of great consequence, the greatest on earth. Impatiently, sadly and with a searching expression, Nadenka looked into my face, responding absent-mindedly as she waited, wondering if I'd speak. Oh, what a play of expression on that dear face, what indeed! I saw her struggle with herself; she had to say something, ask a certain question but couldn't find words, was ill at ease, alarmed, disturbed by joy. . . .

"Do you know something?" she said, not looking at me.

"What?" I asked.

"Let's do it once more . . . slide down."

We climbed the steps to the hill top. Again I seated Nadenka, pale and trembling, in the sledge and again we hurtled down into the terrifying abyss; the wind roared again and the runners whirred, and again, when noise and speed were fiercest, I whispered:

"I love you, Nadia!"

As the sledge came to a halt, Nadenka glanced back at the

hill we'd sped down and then looked a long time into my face and listened intently to my indifferent and impassive voice; and everything about her, even her muff and hood, all of her figure expressed extreme bewilderment.

Her face was saying: "What on earth was it? Who pronounced *those* words? Did he, or did I only seem to hear them?"

The uncertainty made her agitated, put her quite out of patience. The poor girl made no reply to questions and she frowned, on the edge of tears.

"Shall we go home?" I asked.

"But . . . but I like tobogganing . . ." she said, blushing. "Shall we go once again?"

She "liked" tobogganing: all the same, sitting in the sledge, she was pale and trembling, just as before, could scarcely breathe for fear.

We went down for the third time and I saw how she looked into my face, watching my lips. But I put a handkerchief to my lips and coughed, and when we were half way down, I managed to murmur:

"I love you, Nadia!"

And so the enigma was enigma still. Nadenka was silent, pre-occupied. . . .

I saw her home from the rink. She endeavoured to move more quietly, slowing her steps and never ceasing to wonder whether I'd speak those words. And I saw how her spirit was troubled and what control she had to exercise to keep from saying:

"It can't really be the wind that spoke those words. And I don't want it to be the wind!"

Next morning I received a note: "If you're going today to the rink, then call for me. N."

And from then on I began to go there with Nadenka every day and every time we hurtled down in the sledge I whispered the very same words:

"I love you, Nadia!"

Quickly Nadenka became addicted to the words as if to wine or morphia. She couldn't live without them. It was true that hurtling down the slope was terrifying from the very first but fear and danger gave peculiar force to fascinating words of love which from the very first remained a strange enigma troubling her soul. There were only two suspects indeed: the wind and I. Which of them confessed their love she did not know, but clearly it was all the same to her. This drinking cup or that, it's all the same if only you get drunk.

For some reason once at midday I went to the rink. Mingling with a crowd, I saw Nadenka go to the hill as if she were looking for me. . . . Then she went timidly up the steps. She was afraid to slide down alone, so afraid. She was white as snow and trembled as if she were going to execution. But go she did, her mind made up, without a backward glance.

Clearly she had decided at last to make the test: would she hear those wonderfully sweet words if I were not there?

I saw how, blanching, mouth wide with horror, she sat in the sledge, closed her eyes and with a last farewell to earth set off. "Zzzzzz . . ." zoomed the runners. Whether Nadenka heard the words I do not know. I only saw how weak and exhausted she was as she got out of the sledge. And her face showed clearly that she herself did not know if she heard anything or not. Her fear as she swept down took away her power to hear, to distinguish sounds and understand. . . .

But then March was upon us and Spring. The sun grew warmer, our icy slope darkened, losing its sheen and finally melted away. We stopped tobogganing. There was nowhere anymore for poor Nadenka to hear those words, nor anyone to say them either, for the wind was silent and I was going to Petersburg, for a long time, perhaps forever.

It happened that before I left, a couple of days before, I was sitting at twilight in a little garden separated from the place where Nadenka lived by a high nailed fence. It was cold enough still, snow still about by the muck heap and the trees dead; but Spring was in the air for all that, and rooks cawed loudly as they settled to their nests at nightfall. I went up to the fence and looked a long time through a crack. . . .

I watched as Nadenka came out on the porch and turned a mournful, yearning glance at the sky. . . . The spring wind blew straight into her pale, dejected face. . . . It reminded her of the wind that roared at us on the slope when she heard those four words, and her face went sad, most sad, a tear running on her cheek. . . . And the poor girl stretched out both arms as if imploring the wind to bring those words again. And with the wind I whispered:

"I love you, Nadia!"

My God, the effect on her! She cried out, smiled with all her face and stretched her arms into the wind, delighted, joyful, so beautiful.

And I went to pack. . . .

That was all a long time ago. Nadenka is married now: they gave her or she gave herself—it's all the same—to a secretary for wardship of estates and she's three children already. But she's not forgotten how she went with me to the rink and how the wind carried the words, "I love you, Nadia!" It is now the happiest, most endearing and beautiful memory of her life. . . .

And now, as I've grown older, I really don't know why I said those words, for what reason I played the trick.

In the Dark
1886

A FLY OF average size got into the nose of Gagin, assistant
procurator and auxiliary adviser. Curiosity drove it or perhaps it dropped in there by chance or because it was dark; but
the nose couldn't put up with a foreign body and gave the signal
to sneeze. Gagin sneezed, he sneezed with feeling and with such
a piercing wheeze and so loudly that the bed winced with the
sound of shaken springs.

Gagin's wife, Maria Mikhailovna, a big, plump blonde, winced
as well and woke up. She peered into the dark, sighed and turned
on her other side. Five minutes later she turned back again and
shut her eyes more tightly but now sleep wouldn't come. Breathing deeply and stirring from side to side, she raised herself a little,
climbed over her husband, put on her slippers and went to the
window.

It was dark in the yard. Only the silhouettes of trees could
be seen and the dark roof of a shed. The east was slightly, very
slightly lightening but black clouds were gathering over that
light. In the sleepy air, blanketed with mist, there was silence.
Even the house watchman was quiet, paid as he was to break
the nightly silence with his knocking; and quiet too was the
landrail, the only wild bird not to shun the company of summer
visitors in their *dachas*.

Maria Mikhailovna herself broke the silence. Standing at the
window and looking into the yard, she gave a sudden cry. From
the garden with its gaunt, clipped poplar a dark figure of some

sort seemed to be making its way towards the house. At first she thought it a cow or a horse but then, straining her eyes, she clearly distinguished a human shape.

And then the dark figure seemed to her to reach the kitchen window, stop a moment, clearly hesitant, put one foot on the ledge and climb in.

"Thief!" flashed across her mind and a deathly pallor came on her face.

In an instant her imagination drew the picture that people in the *dachas* fear so much: a thief creeping into the kitchen, through the kitchen and into the dining room . . . silverware in the cupboard . . . then the bedroom . . . an axe . . . a villainous face . . . valuables. . . .

Her knees gave way and shivers ran across her back.

"Vasha!" She plucked at her husband. "Basil! Vassili Prokofitch! Oh, my God, he's like a dead man! Wake up, Basil, I implore you!"

"We . . . well?"

The assistant procurator gulped in air, made chewing noises and moaned.

"Wake up, for God's sake! A thief's broken into our kitchen. I was standing at the window and I saw somebody climb in. He'll go through from the kitchen to the dining room. . . . There are spoons in the cupboard! Basil! Last year at Mavra Yegorovna's they broke in just like that."

"Who . . . who is it . . . you want?"

"Oh, my God, he doesn't hear! You realise, don't you, you waxwork, that I've just seen some man climb into our kitchen! Pelegea will be frightened . . . and there's silverware in the cupboard!"

"Rubbish!"

"Basil, this is intolerable! I tell you we're in danger and you sleep and moan! What do you want, then? Do you want them to rob and kill us?"

The assistant procurator slowly raised himself, sat on the bed and filled the air with yawns.

"The devil knows your sort for what you are!" he mumbled. "Can't I even have any peace at night? Waking people up for nothing!"

"But I swear to you, Basil, I saw a man climb in at the window!"

"Well, what about it? Let him climb in. . . . Most probably it's that fireman of Pelegea's who's come to see her."

"Wh . . . what? What did you say?"

"I said it's Pelegea's fireman who's come to see her."

"That's even worse!" cried Maria Mikhailovna. "That's worse than if he's a thief! I won't tolerate cynical goings-on in my own house!"

"Oh, how virtuous, just look! 'I won't tolerate cynical goings-on!' Well, what's it amount to? Without spouting foreign words? From time immemorial, oh Mother Mine, it's been the way of things, sanctified by tradition. And because he's a fireman, he comes in to see our cook."

"No, Basil! This means you don't know me. I can't abide the thought that in my house a thing of that sort . . . a thing like that. . . . Kindly go to the kitchen this minute and tell him to be off! This very minute! And tomorrow I'll tell Pelegea that she can't take liberties of that sort here! When I die, you may put up with cynical behaviour in your own house but now you can't! Kindly go!"

"The devil!" muttered Gagin angrily. "Go on, judge things with your microscopic female mind, why should I go into it?"

"Basil, I'm going to faint!"

Gagin spat, put on his slippers, spat again and set off for the kitchen. It was as dark as inside a barrel with the bung in, and the assistant procurator had to grope along. On the way he felt for the nursery door and woke the nurse.

"Vassilissa," he said, "you took my dressing gown to clean yesterday. Where is it?"

"I gave it to Pelegea, sir, for her to clean."

"What a mess! Taking things away and putting nothing in their place. . . . 'Kindly go about without a dressing gown, will you!'"

Reaching the kitchen, he made for the place where Pelegea slept, on a chest under the saucepan shelf.

"Pelegea!" he began, feeling for her shoulder and tapping it. "You there! Pelegea! Well, what are you up to? Not asleep I see! Who's been creeping in to you through the window?"

"H'm. . . . I beg your pardon. . . . Creeping in through the window! Creeping in to who . . . ?"

"Oh yes, you know about it. . . . The dark keeps nothing hid! Better tell that ruffian of yours to clear off while he's a whole skin! You hear? There's nothing for him here!"

"Have you gone and lost your wits, sir? I beg your pardon. . . . Coming looking for that sort of nonsense. . . . Here day after day you work and worry, run about, get no peace, and then at night you've that sort of talk. . . . You live on four roubles a month . . . for your tea and your sugar, and except for that sort of talk you get no credit from anyone. . . . I lived with tradespeople, I put up with no shame of that sort there."

"Now, now. . . . No good singing that song! Get your fancy fellow out of here this minute! You hear?"

"It's sinful of you, master!" said Pelegea, the sound of tears in her voice. "Gentry. . . . Fine people . . . and no idea at all of the grief we have . . . of our miserable life . . ."

She burst into tears.

"We can be insulted. No one sticks up for us."

"Now, now. . . . It's really all the same to me, you know. The mistress sent me. As for me, well, if he comes in at the window, let him, all the same to me."

It only remained for the assistant procurator to confess he was wrong to question her like that and go back to his wife.

"Listen, Pelegea," he said. "You took my dressing gown to clean it. Where is it?"

"Oh forgive me, sir. I forgot to lay it on the chair. It's hanging on the nail by the stove. . . ."

Gagin groped for the dressing gown by the stove, put it on, and set off quietly to the bedroom.

When her husband went out, Maria Mikhailovna lay down in

bed and began waiting. For three minutes she was calm but
then anxiety started to plague her.

"But how long he's taking!" she thought. "It's all very well if
it's that . . . cynical fellow, but what if it's a thief?"

And again her imagination drew a picture: her husband moving into the dark kitchen . . . a blow from a blunt instrument . . .
dying, unable to utter a sound . . . pool of blood . . .

Five minutes passed, five and a half, six. . . . Cold sweat broke
out on her brow.

"Basil!" she screamed. "Basil!"

"Now what are you shouting for? I'm here. . . ." She heard
her husband's voice and footsteps. "Are they knifing you or what?"

The assistant procurator reached the bed and sat down on
the edge.

"Nobody there at all," he said. "You imagined it, you crack-
pot! . . . You can rest easy, that little goose of yours, Pelegea,
well, she's as virtuous as her mistress is. What a frightened funk
you are! What a . . ."

And the assistant procurator began to tease his wife. He had
livened up, was no longer sleepy.

"What a frightened funk!" He laughed. "Better be off to the
doctor tomorrow and have treatment for hallucinations. You're
a psychopath!"

"There's a smell of tar. . . ." said his wife. "Tar or . . . something like it . . . onion . . . leeks . . ."

"H'm . . . yes. Something of the sort in the air. . . . . Don't feel
like sleep! Tell you what, I'll light the candle. . . . Where are our
matches? And by the way, I'll show you the photograph of the
procurator of the legal chamber. Yesterday when he said goodbye
to us, he gave a photograph. With his autograph."

Gagin struck a match against the wall and lit the candle. But
before he had taken one step from the bed to get the photograph,
there resounded behind him a piercing and heart-rending cry.
Looking back, he saw staring at him a pair of big female eyes,
wide with astonishment, horror, and rage. . . .

"Did you take off your dressing gown in the kitchen?" she
asked, white-faced.

"What about it?"

"Look at yourself!"

The assistant procurator looked at himself and gasped. Instead of a dressing gown a fireman's cloak dangled from his shoulders. How had it got there?

While he considered this question, his wife drew a new picture in her imagination, horrible, impossible: darkness, silence, a whisper, and then . . . and then . . .

A Little Crime
1887

O N HIS WAY back from his evening stroll Miguev, a collegiate assessor, stopped by a telegraph pole and sighed
deeply. At that very spot, a week ago, in the evening as he was
coming home from his stroll, Agnia, who used to be his housemaid, came up after him and snapped maliciously:

"Just you wait! I'll cook your goose so you'll know what it
means to ruin innocent girls. I'll leave the baby on your doorstep,
I'll go to court, and I'll tell your wife. . . ."

And she wanted him to put five thousand roubles in the bank
in her name. Miguev sighed as he remembered and once again
regretted bitterly the passion of a moment that had brought him
such worry and pain.

Reaching his *dacha,* he sat on the step for a breather. It was
just ten o'clock with a sliver of moon peeping from behind the
clouds and not a soul to be seen in the street or about the *dachas.*
The old people who came there for the summer were already
off to bed and the young ones were walking in the woods.

Feeling in both pockets for a match for his cigarette, Miguev
brought his elbow against something soft and, as he glanced
unthinkingly down under his right elbow, his face contorted
with as much horror as if he'd seen a snake there beside him.

Just up against the door lay a bundle, an oblong-shaped thing
tucked up in what felt like a padded quilt. One end of the bundle
was slightly open and the collegiate assessor, slipping his hand
into it, felt something damp and warm. Horrified, he jumped up

and looked about him like a criminal seeking a way to run from his guards.

"She's gone and left it!" he hissed angrily through his teeth and clenched his fists. "There it is . . . there's . . . my . . . my little crime! Oh God!"

He went cold with fear, anger and shame. Now what was he to do? What would his wife say if she found out? What would his colleagues say? His Excellency, of course, would dig him in the ribs, chuckle and say: "Congratulations! Ha-ha-ha! . . . Grey hair in your beard but the devil's down below! You rascal, Semeon Erastovitch!" All the neighbours would know his secret now and respectable mothers of families, very probably, would turn him from their doors. They reported such things in the papers and so the humble name of Miguev would go all over Russia. . . .

The middle window of the *dacha* was open and he clearly heard his wife, Anna Filipovna, laying the table for supper; in the yard, just inside the gate, Yermolai, the watchman, was mournfully strumming his balalaika. Let the baby only wake up and squeal and his secret was known. Miguev felt an overpowering desire to do something quickly.

"Get a move on," he muttered, "a move on! This minute while no-one's looking. I'll take it somewhere, set it down on someone else's porch. . . ."

Miguev picked up the bundle in one hand and quietly, with steady step lest he arouse suspicion, went down the street.

"What an astonishing mess to be in!" he thought, trying to assume a look of unconcern. "A collegiate assessor going down the street with a baby! Oh God, if anyone sees and realises what it's all about, I'm sunk.

"I'll put it on this doorstep. . . . No, wait, the window's open, someone might be looking out. Where shall I put it? Ah, I know what, I'll take it to the *dacha* of Melkin, the merchant. Merchants are rich people and good-hearted; they might say thank you and adopt it.

And Miguev decided to take the child at once to Melkin's, although the merchant's *dacha* was on the last street of all, by the river side.

114

"If only he doesn't start screaming or wriggling out of the bundle!" thought the collegiate assessor. "Well, here we are: thank you very much, what a surprise! I'm carrying a human being under my arm like a briefcase. A human being with a soul and feelings like all the rest of us. If he's lucky and the Melkins adopt him, he may very likely turn out to be somebody. Very likely turn out to be a professor of some sort, a general, a writer. Anything's possible in this world! Now I'm carrying him under my arm like some old rubbish, but in thirty years or forty, very likely, I'll have to stand to attention when I see him. . . ."

As Miguev went by a long row of fences along a narrow alley deserted under thick shadows of lime trees, it suddenly seemed to him he was doing something cruel and wrong.

"That's what it is, when you look at it, mean! So mean you can't think of anything meaner. Why am I carting this unhappy child from door to door? Is it his fault he's been born? What harm's he done me? We're all scoundrels! We like to go on the spree but the innocent babies have to foot the bill. It's sickening to think of all this mess. I've been dissolute and now this child has a grim fate in store. If I leave him at the Melkins', they'll put him in an orphanage, among strangers all the time, always tied by regulations . . . no love, no affection, no cuddling. . . . They'll apprentice him then to a shoemaker. He'll take to drink and foul language, pine with hunger. . . . A shoemaker, but the son of a collegiate assessor, of good family. My flesh and blood! . . ."

Miguev came from the shadows of the lime trees to the bright moonlight of the road, unwrapped the bundle and looked at the baby.

"Asleep!" he murmured. "Well, how do you like that, the rascal's a hooked nose like his father? Asleep with no inkling that his father's looking at him. . . . It's a drama, old friend. . . . well, forgive me. . . . Please forgive me, old friend. . . . Seems you were born to this. . . ."

The collegiate assessor blinked and felt a kind of shiver over his cheeks. . . . He wrapped up the baby, put him under his arm and strode forward. All along the way, right up to the Melkins' *dacha*, moral questions worried his head and conscience plagued him.

"If I were a decent and honourable man," he thought, "I wouldn't give a damn. I'd take this little lad to Anna Filipovna, kneel to her and say: 'Forgive me, I'm a sinner. Tear me to shreds but we won't ruin this innocent child. We've no children, let's adopt him.' She's a good sort, she'd agree. And then I'd have my child with me. . . . Eh!"

He reached the Melkins' *dacha* and hesitated. . . .

He imagined himself sitting in the parlour at home, reading the paper while a little boy with a hooked nose played with the tassel of his dressing gown; but at the same time he pictured his colleagues winking and His Excellency digging him in the ribs and chuckling. . . . As well as qualms of conscience he felt a kind of tenderness, affection and sadness. . . .

The collegiate assessor carefully laid the child on the porch step and flapped his hand. . . . Again he felt a kind of shiver across his face.

"Forgive me, old friend. I'm a scoundrel!" he muttered. "Don't think badly of me!"

He stepped a pace back but immediately gave a determined grunt and said:

"Oh, come what may, I don't give a damn! I'm taking him, let people say what they like!"

Miguev picked up the baby and hurried back.

"Let them say what they like," he thought. "I'll go in right away, kneel down and say: 'Anna Filipovna.' She's a good sort, she'll understand. . . . And we'll bring him up. If it's a boy, we'll call him Vladimir, Anna, if it's a girl. A comfort for us he or she will be in our old age. . . ."

And he did just as he'd decided. Weeping, near to fainting with shame and fear, full of hope and a diffuse delight, he went into the *dacha* to his wife and fell on his knees before her. . . .

"Anna Filipovna," he said, sobbing and laying the baby on the floor. "Don't condemn me before you hear me. I'm a sinner. This is my child. . . . You remember Agnia, to be sure. . . . The devil tempted me to it. . . ."

And beside himself with fear and shame he didn't wait for a reply but jumped to his feet and ran like a beaten dog into the open air.

"I'll stay out in the yard till she calls me," he thought, "give her time to come to her senses and think it over. . . ."

Yermolai, the watchman, went by with his balalaika, glanced at him and shrugged his shoulders. A minute later he came by again and again he shrugged.

"Here's a funny how-do-you-do!" he muttered, grinning. "And no mistake! Aksinia, the washerwoman, was here just now, Semeon Erastovitch. Like a fool she put her baby on the steps here and came in with me for a bit . . . and somebody's been up and off with it. . . . Fancy that!"

"What? What's that you say?" shouted Miguev at the top of his voice.

Yermolai, attributing his master's anger to a different cause, scratched his head and sighed.

"Sorry, Semeon Erastovitch," he said, "but it's the summer holiday time . . . and you can't get by without it . . . without a woman, I mean. . . ."

And seeing his master's eyes staring with such bitter astonishment, he cleared his throat guiltily and went on:

"It's a sin, of course, but what can you do? You won't let us have strange women in the house, that's a fact, but where are we to get any of our own? . . . Before, when little Agnia was living here, I didn't have any strange women in, because there was one here for me . . . but nowadays, well, you can see yourself, sir . . . you can't manage without a woman. . . . But when little Agnia was here, there was no breaking rules because . . ."

"Get out, you scoundrel!" shouted Miguev, stamped his feet and went back into the room.

Anna Filipovna, astonished and angry, was sitting in the same place, on the edge of tears, not taking her eyes off the baby.

"Now, now . . ." muttered Miguev, pale, twisting his mouth into a smile. "I was joking. . . . It's not mine . . . but the washerwoman's. . . . I was joking. . . . Take it to the watchman."

Volodya
1887

A T FIVE O'CLOCK on a Sunday afternoon in summer, Volodya, seventeen years old, ugly, ailing and shy, sat gloomily in the Shumihins' summer-house, depressed by several things.

In the first place, he had to sit a math examination the next morning and they'd expel him if he couldn't do the written problems: he'd been already two years in the sixth form and his yearly algebra grading was only two and three quarters.

Secondly, the Shumihins were rich and liked to think themselves aristocrats and every time that he and *Maman* came to stay with them, his pride was hurt. Madame Shumihin and her nieces seemed to treat them like poor relations and slighted and made fun of *Maman*: once on the terrace he overheard Madame Shumihin talking about her to her cousin Anna Fedorovna, saying she pretended to be younger than she was and painted herself, never paid her debts at cards and had a weakness for other people's bootees and tobacco. Every day he implored *Maman* not to visit them, insisting it was degrading to curry favour with people like that; he was forceful, even rude, but she, spoilt and empty-headed, having squandered two fortunes, her own and his father's, still hankered after high society and just didn't understand. So twice a week he had to come here, to this cursed *dacha*.

And thirdly, he couldn't for a minute thrust off a strange unpleasant feeling, something quite new. . . .

Yes, he must be in love with Madame Shumihin's cousin and guest, Anna Fedorovna: a married woman, vivacious, loud-voiced and quick to laugh; thirty years old, lusty and sturdy, rosy-cheeked, with plump shoulders and a round chin, her dainty lips always smiling. Not beautiful and not young. He knew that very well yet couldn't stop thinking of her or looking as she shrugged her sleek shoulders, her smooth back moving, at a croquet stroke, or even as she fell into a chair after a bout of laughter or a rush on the stairs, screwing up her eyes and gasping as if her breasts were cramped and stifled.

And she had a husband, a sedate architect who came once a week to the *dacha,* slept soundly and then went back to town. Volodya's strange feeling had begun with a hatred for this architect, altogether irrational, and a sudden joy whenever he went away.

And now, sitting in the summer-house and worrying about to-morrow's examination and the way they made fun of *Maman,* he felt an overpowering desire to see Nouta—as the Shumihins called Anna Fedorovna—and to hear her laughter and the rustle of her dress. . . .

It was a desire that had nothing to do with the pure romantic love he read about in novels and dreamed of as he went to sleep. It was strange and hard to understand; and it made him ashamed like something ugly and coarse he feared to admit was his own. . . .

"This isn't love," he told himself. "You don't fall in love with married women of thirty. You have affairs with them, that's all. . . ."

This thought made him remember how painfully shy he was, that he'd freckles and narrow eyes and couldn't grow a moustache; and he imagined himself beside Nouta. But to see them together like that was so hard that he had to pretend he was good-looking, daring, witty and dressed in the very latest style.

Deep in these dreams, hunched over, staring at the ground, in a dark corner of the summer-house, he heard light steps. Someone was sauntering along the path. Suddenly the steps paused and something white glimmered in the doorway.

119

"Is anybody there?"

A feminine voice that he recognized as Nouta's; startled, he looked up.

"Who's there?" asked Nouta, coming in. "Oh, it's you, Volodya? What are you doing here? Brooding? How do you manage to keep on brooding and brooding. That's the way people go mad."

Volodya got up and stared bewilderedly at Nouta. She'd just come from the bath house, a rough towel and a sheet about her shoulders, little locks of hair curling out under a white silk turban and sticking to her forehead. A damp, cool smell of bathing and almond-scented soap came wafting from her. She was breathless from the exercise and the top button of her blouse was undone so that he saw her neck and breasts.

"Why so silent, then?" she asked, looking him up and down. "That's bad manners when a lady speaks to you. But you're so uncouth, Volodya. You sit around all day brooding and pondering like some sort of philosopher. There's no life in you, no fire. You're a stodgy piece of work, you really are. At your age you should be sprightly, on the move, doing some courting, falling in love."

Volodya stared at the sheet held by her plump white hand and thought. . . .

"Not a sound!" said Nouta with surprise. "How funny. . . !"

"Listen," she went on. "Be a man! Come on, give us a smile! Ugh, you stodgy little philosopher!"

She burst out laughing.

"Do you know, Volodya, why you're so uncouth? It's because you don't flirt with ladies. Why don't you? Of course there isn't a girl here, I know, but why not flirt with a married woman? Why not flirt with me, eh?"

Volodya listened and, tense with brooding concentration, scratched his temple.

"It's only proud people who are so silent and keep aloof," went on Nouta, snatching his hand away from his temple. "You're proud, Volodya. Why are your eyes so sullen? Please look me in the face! Oh, what an uncouth chap!"

Volodya decided he had to speak. Trying to smile, he twitched

120

his lower lip, blinked and once again plucked at his temple.

"I . . . I love you!" he said.

Nouta frowned in amazement and burst out laughing.

"What's this I hear?"—She trilled like an opera singer as a messenger brings devastating news—"What? What did you say? Say it again. Go on, again."

"I . . . I love you!" Volodya repeated.

And automatically, without intent or even understanding, he stepped half a pace towards her and clutched her arm above the wrist. Tears blurred his eyes and ran down, all his world narrowing to a big, rough towel with a smell of the bath house.

"Bravo! Bravo!"—He heard a hearty chuckle—"Why so silent, then? I want to hear you speak to me. Come on."

Aware that nothing stopped him taking her arm, he stared at Nouta's laughing face and clumsily and jerkily put both his arms around her so that his wrists came together across her back. He held her waist with both hands as she lifted her dimpled arms to pat in place her hair under the turban at the neck.

"Volodya," she murmured, "you have to be gentle, charming and know what you're about, and only being with ladies can teach you that. But you've such a coarse . . . and well, a spiteful face. You have to speak nicely, smile. . . . Yes, Volodya, you mustn't be surly, you're young and you've lots of time to be a philosopher. . . . But let me go. I must be off. Let me go, I say."

With little effort she freed her waist and humming something, went out of the summer-house.

Volodya stayed where he was, smoothing down his hair and smiling, then paced three times from corner to corner. After that he sat on a bench and smiled again. He felt so terribly ashamed it surprised him even that human shame could have such bitterness and force. It was shame that was making him smile, making him mutter incoherently and fling his arms about.

He was ashamed of being treated like a little boy, ashamed of his shyness, but most of all ashamed of having the effrontery to clutch a respectable married woman round the waist when neither his age, his qualities nor his social position gave him the right.

He jumped up and left the summer-house and without a

glance to left or right walked deep in the garden away from the house.

"The quicker I get out of this place the better!"—he clutched his head—"Oh God, the quicker, the better!"

Volodya and his mother's train left at 8.40. Three hours more, but he'd have been delighted to go to the station there and then, not waiting for *Maman*.

At eight o'clock he approached the house, his every nerve screwed up determinedly: what would be, would be. In spite of everything he'd walk in with a bold face, look straight ahead and speak in loud, clear voice.

He crossed the terrace, the hall, the drawing room, then paused for breath. He heard them taking tea in the nearby dining room, chattering and laughing.

He listened.

"I assure you," Nouta was saying, "I couldn't believe my eyes. And when he began to tell me he was in love and imagine, put his arms around my waist, I didn't recognize him. And, you know, he has a way with him. When he told me he loved me, there was something brutal about him, like a Circassian."

"Really!" gasped *Maman*, as she went off into protracted laughter. "Really! How that reminds me of his father!"

Volodya darted back and ran out into the fresh air.

"How could they talk about it like that, openly?"—He clasped his hands in torment, gazing with horror at the sky—"Openly! In cold blood! And *Maman* laughing. *Maman!* Oh God, why have You given me such a mother, why?"

But he had to go back into the house, at all costs he had to. Three times he walked along the path till he was somewhat calmer, then went in.

"Why didn't you come in time for tea?" asked Madame Shumihin severely.

"I'm sorry . . . but it's time to go," he muttered, not lifting his eyes. "*Maman*, it's eight o'clock."

"Go by yourself, my dear," murmured *Maman* languidly. "I'm staying overnight with Lily. Goodbye, love. . . . Come here and let me bless you."

She made the sign of the cross over her son and, turning to Nouta, said in French:

"He looks a little like Lermontov, don't you think?"

Muttering some sort of goodbye and avoiding their faces, Volodya went out. Ten minutes later he was walking along the road to the station and most glad of it: he no longer felt afraid or ashamed and his breath was light and free.

Half a mile or so from the station he sat on a stone by the roadside and gazed at the sun, half-hidden by a bank. Lights were on here and there in the station and a dim green signal glimmered but there was no sign yet of the train. It was pleasant to sit quite still listening to the gradual approach of evening. The dark summer-house, her footsteps, the smell of the bath house wafting from her, her laughter and her waist—they were all there with striking clarity in his imagination but no longer seemed so frightening or important.

"Something and nothing, that's all. She didn't take her hand away and she laughed when I held her in my arms. That shows she liked it. If she hadn't liked it, she'd have been angry. . . ."

And now it annoyed him that in the summer-house he'd not been daring enough. He regretted coming away so foolishly and felt sure that, if he had the chance again, he'd be bolder, see things more simply.

And it wouldn't be difficult to make that happen. After supper at the Shumihins' they walked about for a long time. If he walked with Nouta in the dark garden—well, there was his chance!

"I'll go back," he thought, "and leave tomorrow on the morning train. . . . I'll say I missed the train."

He did go back but Madame Shumihin, *Maman*, Nouta and one of the nieces were sitting on the terrace playing cards. When Volodya told them he missed the train, they were worried about him not being in time for tomorrow's examination and advised him to get up early.

All through their game he sat aside watching and waiting, a plan already formed in his mind: he would go over in the dark to Nouta and take her hand, then put his arms around her.

No need for a word, all understood in quietness between them.

But after supper the ladies didn't go for their walk; they continued their game. They went on playing until it was one o'clock, then broke off to go to bed.

"What a mess!" muttered Volodya as he got into bed. "But never mind. I'll try again tomorrow. Tomorrow in the summerhouse. Never mind. . . ."

He didn't try to sleep but sat up clutching his knees and thinking. The thought of the examination was repugnant. He'd made up his mind they'd expel him and being expelled didn't seem so terrible. On the contrary it was rather good, yes, very good indeed. Tomorrow he'd be free as a bird, put on ordinary clothes, not a school uniform, smoke quite openly and come back here and make love to Nouta when he felt like it. Not a schoolboy any more, a young man.

And as for his career and the future, that was clear enough. He'd volunteer for the army, be a telegraphist, or go into a chemist's shop and work his way up to dispenser. There were lots of professions, weren't there?

An hour passed, two, and still he sat and brooded.

Towards three, just as it was becoming light, the door gave a cautious-sounding creak and *Maman* came in.

"Not sleeping?" she yawned. "Go to sleep. I won't be a` minute. I came for drops, that's all. . . ."

"Why?"

"Poor Lily's had another attack. Sleep, my dear, you've an examination tomorrow. . . ."

She took a bottle from a cupboard, read the label at the window and went out.

A minute later Volodya heard a woman's voice: "These aren't the drops, Maria Leontevna. That's *convallaria*, Lily's asking for morphia. Is your son asleep? Ask him to look. . . ."

It was Nouta's voice. Volodya went cold. He hurriedly pulled on trousers, flung an overcoat over his shoulders and went to the door.

"You understand? Morphia!" Nouta was whispering. "It will be written in Latin. Wake Volodya, he'll find it. . . ."

Maman opened the door and Volodya saw Nouta. She had on the same blouse as when she came from the bath house, her uncombed hair falling about her shoulders, her sleepy face shadowy in the half light.

"Look, Volodya's not asleep," she said. "Volodya, be a dear and look for the morphia in the cupboard. It's shocking with Lily. Always something wrong with her."

Maman muttered something, yawned and went away.

"Go and look, then," said Nouta. "What are you standing there for?"

Volodya went to the cupboard, knelt down and fumbled through the medicine bottles and boxes. His hands trembled and his chest and stomach felt so strange as if cold waves were flowing through him. He snatched with trembling fingers, without rhyme or reason, at ether, carbolic acid and different drugs, spilling them, their smell making him dizzy and out of breath.

"*Maman's* gone, then," he thought. "Good. . . . That's good. . . ."

"Get a move on, will you?" drawled Nouta.

"Rightaway. . . . This is it, I think, morphia . . ." he said, seeing the letters m.o.r.p.h. on a label. "Please take it."

Nouta stood with one foot just inside the room, patting her hair in place—rather difficult, it was so long and thick—and staring dreamily at Volodya. In a billowing blouse, sleepy-eyed, her hair loose-flowing, she seemed to Volodya in the window's pale dawn light most fascinating and splendid. Deeply attracted, trembling in every limb and dazzled by the thought that in the summer-house he'd held this lovely body in his arms, he gave her the bottle and said:

"You're so . . ."

"What?"

She came in, smiling.

"What?"

He was silent, looking at her, then, just as in the summer-house, he took her arm . . . and she looked back at him, smiling and expectant: well, what's coming now?

"I love you . . ." he whispered.

125

THE SINNER FROM TOLEDO AND OTHER STORIES

She stopped smiling, thought a moment, then said:

"Wait, I think someone's coming. . . ."

"Oh, these schoolboys and me!" she murmured as she went to the door and glanced along the corridor. "No, no-one to be seen."

She came back in.

To Volodya it seemed that the room, Nouta, the dawn and he himself merged altogether in a sharp and most strange feeling of fantastic happiness for which you could give up all your life and suffer an eternity of torment . . . but half a minute passed and all this suddenly disappeared. Then he saw only a plump, plain face, distorted by repugnance . . . and he felt a sudden bitter aversion for all that had happened.

"I'll have to go, you know," said Nouta, looking him up and down with scorn. "What a nasty little chap you are! Ugh, you ugly duckling!"

How loathsome now seemed her long hair and floppy blouse, her walk, her voice!

"Ugly duckling!" he thought, as she went out. "I am ugly! Everything's ugly!"

The sun was coming up over the courtyard, birds sang loudly and he heard the steps of the gardener, the creak of his wheelbarrow. . . .

A little later came the mooing of cows, the notes of a shepherd's pipe. . . .

The sun's light and those sounds told him that somewhere on earth a pure and graceful and artistic life existed. But where? Neither his mother nor any of the people who surrounded him spoke a word about such things.

When the servant came to wake him for the morning train, he pretended to be asleep.

"Oh, the devil with it all!"

He got up at eleven. Brushing his hair at the mirror and looking at his graceless face pasty from lack of sleep, he thought:

"Quite true: an ugly duckling!"

When his mother was horrified he wasn't at the examination,

he said: "I overslept, *Maman*. But don't worry. I'll hand in a doctor's certificate."

Madame Shumihin and Nouta stayed in bed till one o'clock. He heard Madame Shumihin thrust open her window as she woke and Nouta respond to her harsh voice with a hoot of laughter. Later, when the door opened and they all trooped in for lunch, the nieces and the various hangers-on and *Maman* among them, he noticed how Nouta's washed face shone as she laughed, beside it the black brows and beard of the architect who had just arrived.

She had on a Little-Russian costume which was quite unsuitable and made her look clumsy; the architect cracked stale and vulgar jokes; and there seemed far too much onion in the rissoles. And it seemed too that Nouta was laughing loudly on purpose and glancing scornfully towards him as if to show him that memory of the night's events gave her no concern and she did not notice at the table the presence of an ugly duckling.

At four o'clock he went with *Maman* to the station. Grim memories, his sleepless night, the coming expulsion and a pang of conscience stirred in him a bitter and dark anger. He stared at his mother's gaunt profile and her little skinny nose, then at the mackintosh that Nouta had given her and muttered:

"Why do you powder your face? It's awful at your age. You paint yourself, you never pay your debts at cards and you cadge tobacco. It's disgusting. I don't like you! No, I don't!"

He was insulting her and she glanced about in alarm, clasped her hands and whispered, horrified:

"What is it, dear? My God, the coachman will hear! Do be quiet or the coachman will hear! He can hear everything."

"I don't like you. . . . No, I don't. . . ." gasped Volodya. "You're a heartless slut. Don't you dare wear that mackintosh. Listen to me or I'll rip it in pieces. . . ."

"Oh, do control yourself, my darling!" His mother began to cry. "The coachman can hear."

"And what's become of father's fortune? Where's your money? You've squandered it. I'm not ashamed of being poor but I'm ashamed that I've a mother like you. Whenever my friends ask about you, I blush."

The train had to pass two stations on the way to town. He stayed out on the platform all the time, trembling from top to toe, for he didn't want to go in a compartment with the mother he despised. He despised himself too, the ticket collectors, the engine smoke, the cold that made him tremble. . . . But the more bitter his mood, the surer he was that somewhere in the world for some people was a life that was pure, noble, warm and graceful, that love was there, tenderness, gaiety and freedom. Yes, he was sure of it, and it made him so sad at heart that a fellow passenger stared at him and asked: "You've toothache, have you?"

In town Volodya and his mother lodged with Maria Petrovna, a lady of high rank who had a large flat and let out parts of it. *Maman* paid her for two rooms, one for herself with a window, a bed and two pictures in gilt frames, and another, next door, small and dark, for Volodya. He had a sofa to sleep on and no other furniture at all. A wicker basket full of clothes, hat boxes and all sorts of his mother's rubbish took up all the space. He did his homework in his mother's room or in the "common lounge" as they called it, the big room where all the lodgers went at dinner time and in the evening.

Once they were home Volodya lay on the sofa and pulled the quilt over him to stop his trembling. The wicker basket, the hat boxes and the rest reminded him that he hadn't a place of his own, no refuge from *Maman* and the lodgers' voices coming up from the common lounge; and his satchel and books made him think of the examination he had missed.

For some reason he remembered Mentone where he lived with his late father when he was seven; and Biarritz and the two little English girls who played with him on the sand.

He tried to bring into memory the colour of the sky, the ocean, the high waves and his feelings at that time but he couldn't manage it. The English girls flickered in his imagination as if alive, the rest diffused and blurred.

"No," he thought, "it's cold here!"

He got up, put on his overcoat and went to the common lounge.

They were drinking tea there, three of them by the samovar: *Maman*, the music teacher, an old woman with tortoise-shell *pince-nez*, and Augustin Mihalitch, a very fat, elderly Frenchman who worked in a perfume-making factory.

"I've had no dinner today," his mother was saying. "We'll have to send the housemaid out for bread."

"Dunyasha!" shouted the Frenchman.

It seemed the landlady had sent the maid off somewhere.

"It doesn't matter," said the Frenchman with a broad smile. "I'll go for bread myself at once. Oh, it's nothing!"

He set down his strong, pungent cigar in a prominent place, put on his hat and went out. As soon as he had gone, *Maman* began to tell the music teacher that she'd been a guest of the Shumihins and how warmly they'd welcomed her.

"Lily Shumihin is a relative of mine, you know," she said. "Her late husband General Shumihin was my husband's cousin. And she herself was born Baroness Kolb. . . ."

"That's not true, *Maman*," snapped Volodya. "Why are you telling lies?"

He knew very well his mother was speaking the truth. It was correct, all she said about General Shumihin and Baroness Kolb, and yet he felt sure she was lying. Deceit was there in her tone, her expression, her eyes, everything.

"You're lying!" he repeated, thumping the table with such force that cups and saucers shook and *Maman*'s tea was spilt. "Why do you talk about a general and a baroness. It's all lies!"

The startled music teacher coughed into her handkerchief, pretending to be sneezing, and *Maman* burst into tears.

"Where can I go?" thought Volodya.

He had been in the street already and was too ashamed to call on friends.

Again without rhyme or reason came the memory of the two English girls. . . .

He strode from corner to corner of the common lounge and

129

went out into Augustin Mihalitch's room. There was a strong smell of medicinal oil and soap of glycerine and on the table, the window sills and even chairs were bottles and glasses of many-coloured liquids. . . .

Volodya took a newspaper from the table, unfolded it and looked at the heading: *Figaro.* . . . It had a strong and rather pleasant smell. . . .

Then from the table he took up a revolver. . . .

"Now, now, dear. Don't you pay any attention."

The music teacher was consoling *Maman* in the next room. "He's still so young. At his age they always take liberties. We have to reconcile ourselves to it."

"No, Eugenia Andrevna," wailed his mother in a sing-song voice, "he's too spoiled. There's no man to look after him and I'm weak and can't do it. Oh, I'm wretched!"

Volodya put the muzzle of the revolver in his mouth, felt something like a trigger or spring and squeezed it with his finger. He found something that jutted out and squeezed that. . . .

He took the revolver from his mouth, wiped it on the flap of his overcoat and examined the lock. It was the first time he'd held a firearm in his hand. . . .

"It looks as though you have to lift up this thing . . ." he muttered. "Yes . . . that's what it looks like. . . ."

Augustin Mihalitch came into the lounge chuckling and telling some tale or other.

Volodya put the muzzle in his mouth again, gripping it with his teeth, then squeezed something with his finger.

A shot rang out. . . .

Something struck Volodya with fearful force at the back of his head and he fell across the table, his face among the bottles and glasses.

He saw his father, just as he was in Mentone, a big broad ribbon round his top hat in memory of some lady who had died; he clasped him suddenly with both hands and they flew, the two of them, towards some dark and very deep abyss.

Then all blurred and disappeared.

A Tale without a Title
1888

IN THE FIFTH CENTURY, just as now, the sun rose each
morning and each evening sank to rest. In the morning, as
first rays glanced on dew, earth came to life and air was full
of noises of delight and hope but in the evening this same earth
went quiet, shrouded in stern dark. Day was like day, night like
night.

At times clouds lowered and thunder roared or a star lost
its way and fell from the sky or a white-faced monk ran and
told his brothers he had seen a tiger not far from the monastery—
only things of that sort and then once again day was like day,
night like night.

The monks worked and prayed to God and their Father
Superior played the organ, wrote Latin verses and composed
music. This wonderful old man had an extraordinary gift. He
played the organ with such skill that even very old monks,
their hearing dulled by age, could not hold back their tears as
the sounds reached them from his cell. When he spoke of something, even very ordinary, like trees or animals or the sea, it
was impossible to listen without a smile or a tear for it seemed
the same chords sounded in his nature as within the organ.

If he became angry or yielded to strong joy or began to
speak of something terrible or wonderful, a passionate inspiration came upon him, tears fell from his shining eyes, his voice
was like thunder, and the monks who listened felt his inspiration
hold them spellbound. In those magnificent, wonderful moments

his power over them was infinite and if he had ordered them to throw themselves into the sea, they would have rushed, even to the last of them, to carry out his wishes.

His praise of God, of heaven and earth in music, verse and song was for the monks a source of unfailing joy. Trees, flowers, spring and autumn might be dull in their monotonous life, the roar of the sea be weary to their ears, birdsong be an irritant, but the talents of their Father Superior, like wholesome bread, were necessary every day.

Dozens of years went by and always day was like day, night like night. Except for wild birds and beasts not a soul came near the monastery. The closest place of human habitation was a long way off and to reach it from the monastery, or the monastery from it, you had to cross some seventy miles of desert. Only those who cut themselves off from a life they despised made up their minds to cross the desert, coming to the monastery as to the grave.

So the monks were very surprised when one night there knocked at the gate someone who seemed a man of the city and a very ordinary sinner relishing life. Instead of asking the Father's blessing and praying, this man demanded wine and food. When they asked him how he came to leave the city for the desert, he told them a long hunter's tale: he set out, drank too much and lost his way. When they suggested he become a monk to save his soul, he answered with a smile:

"I'm no mate for you."

As he ate and drank, he watched the monks who served him, shook his head reproachfully and said:

"You do nothing, you monks. You just eat and drink, you know. Do you really save a soul that way? Think. While you sit here content, eating and drinking and dreaming of salvation, your fellow men are dying off and going to hell. Take a look at what's going on in the city! Some are dying of hunger while others, not knowing what to do with their gold, sing in debauchery and die like flies stuck in honey. There's no faith in people nor truth! Well, whose job is it to save them? Whose job is it to preach to them? Is it mine, when I'm drunk from morning till night? Did God really give you faith, a humble spirit and a loving heart for you to sit here between four walls and do nothing?"

His drunken words were impudent and unseemly but they had a strange effect on the Father Superior. The old man glanced from one monk to another, went pale and said:

"Yes, brothers, he is speaking the truth! Poor people are indeed dying by folly and weakness in sin and atheism, and we do not move from this place as if it did not concern us. Why should I not go and remind them of the Christ they have forgotten?"

The words of the man from the city obsessed the Father Superior; the very next day he took his staff, said goodbye to the brothers and set off for the city. And the monks were bereft of his music, his speeches and verses.

A dull month passed, another, but the old man did not return. Then at the end of the third month they heard the well-known tap of his staff. The monks rushed out to meet him, showering him with questions but instead of rejoicing to see them he wept bitterly and did not say a single word. The monks noticed he had greatly aged and withered: his face was weary and looked very sad and, as he wept, he seemed a man who has suffered outrage.

The monks began to weep as he did and gently asked the reason for his weeping and why his face was so morose but he spoke no word and shut himself up in his cell. For seven days he stayed there, weeping, neither eating nor drinking nor playing the organ. If the monks knocked at his door or asked him to come out and share his sorrows with them, his response was deep silence.

At last he came out. Gathering all the monks about him, he began with tear-stained face and looks of grief and anger to tell what happened to him in those last three months. His voice was tranquil and his eyes smiled as he described his journey from the monastery to the city. As he went along, he said, birds sang to him, streams murmured and sweet youthful hopes excited his spirits; he walked feeling like a soldier going into battle, confident of victory; he dreamed as he walked, composing verses and hymns and did not notice when his journey ended.

But his voice faltered, his eyes flashed and all his being burned with anger when he began to speak of the city and its people. Never in his life had he seen nor even dared to imagine what he encountered entering the city. Only there, for the first time in his life, in old age, did he see and understand the power of the devil and the fascination of evil and how weak and cowardly and worthless people were.

By unhappy chance the first house he entered was that of a debauchee. Some fifty men and women of great wealth were eating and drinking out of all proportion. Intoxicated with wine they sang songs and brazenly spoke terrible repulsive words that no man fearing God dare think of saying; free beyond measure, gay and happy, they feared neither God, devil nor death but said and did all they wished and went wherever their lust directed. The wine, clear as amber, flickering with golden flashes, was, it seemed, unbearably sweet and fragrant, for all who drank it smiled with happiness and longed to drink again. And the wine smiled back as the men smiled and sparkled joyfully as they drank, as if it knew the evil fascination hidden in its sweetness.

The old man, more incensed and with tears of indignation, went on to describe what he saw. On a table, in the midst of the revellers, he said, stood a half-naked harlot. It was hard to imagine or find in nature anything more lovely and fascinating. This vile creature, young, long-haired and swarthy, dark-eyed, plump-lipped, shameless and brazen, bared her snow-white teeth and smiled as if she wished to say: "Look, how vicious I am, how lovely!"

Silk and brocade slipped down in lovely folds from her shoulders but her beauty did not want the covering of clothes but burst our avidly through folds like young grass from spring earth. The brazen woman drank wine, sang songs and gave herself to all who wanted her.

Shaking his arms in anger, the old man then described chariot races, bull fights, theatres and studios where artists painted naked women or moulded them in clay. He spoke with inspiration, beautifully, resoundingly, as if playing on unseen chords, and the petrified monks listened greedily, engrossed in his words and sighing with rapture.

Having described all the charms of the devil, the fascination of evil and the captivating grace of the loathsome female body, the old man cursed the devil, turned away and closed behind him the door of his cell.

When he came out next morning, not a monk was left in the monastery. They were all hurrying to the city.

The Women
1891

IN THE VILLAGE of Raybuzh, just opposite the church, stands a two-storied stone house with an iron roof. The owner, Philip Ivanov Kashin, known as Doudya, lives with his family on the ground floor, and upstairs, where it is very cold in winter and very hot in summer, civil servants, merchants and people of private means lodge for a day or so during their travels.

Doudya rents some plots of land, owns a small pub on the main road, trades in tar, honey, cattle and magpies and has stocked up eight thousand roubles in the city bank.

His elder son, Fedor, is chief engineer in a factory and, as they say, has so gone up in the world you cannot even reach him with your fingertips; his wife, Sophia, a plain and sickly woman, lives with her father-in-law, cries all the time and every Sunday goes to hospital for treatment.

His younger son, "Aleshka the hunchback," lives with his father. Not long ago they picked a wife for him from a poor family: Barbara, young, healthy and pretty and fond of dressing up. When civil servants and merchants are there, it's always her they call for to bring them tea or make their beds.

One June evening, as the sun was going down and the air was heavy with the smell of hay, warm manure and fresh milk, there came into Doudya's courtyard a simple cart with three people in it: a man of thirty or so in a canvas suit beside a lad of seven or eight in a long dark coat with big bone buttons, and a young fellow in a red shirt who was driving.

The latter unharnessed the horses and led them along the road and the older man washed himself, turned to the church and said a prayer, then spread a rug near the cart and sat down to supper with the lad. He ate calmly and slowly and Doudya, who had seen many travellers in his time, recognized in him a merchant who knew his own worth.

Doudya sat bare-headed in his waistcoat on the verandah and waited for the man to speak. Travellers usually talked to him about themselves before turning in and he liked to hear their tales. Afanasevna, his old lady, and Sophia, his daughter-in-law, were milking cows in the shed; and Barbara, his other daughter-in-law, was sitting at an open upstairs window munching sun-flower seeds.

"The boy's your son, I suppose?" said Doudya.

"No. I adopted him. He's an orphan. I did it for my soul's good."

They began to chat. The traveller proved to be a talkative fellow, well able to express himself and Doudya learned that he was Matvei Savitch, middle class and from the town, now on his way to inspect some orchards that he leased from German settlers, and that the lad was called Kouska.

The evening was so warm and sultry that nobody felt like turning in, and, as it darkened, pale stars beginning to twinkle somewhere above, Matvei Savitch told how he came to adopt the boy. Afanasevna and Sophia stood some distance away to listen and Kouska himself went off to the gate.

"Well, old man, it's a complicated story," began Matvei Savitch, "and if I told you it all, just as it was, well, we'd be here all night or longer. Ten years ago in my street, in the very house that stands next to mine, in fact—today it's a tallow and oil factory —there lived an old widow, Marfa Simonovna Kaplunzev, and her two sons. The older one was a guard on the railway and the other, Vasha, who was my age, stayed at home with her.

"Their late father had five pairs of horses and employed car- riers and draymen up and down the town. His widow kept the business on—she could control the men as well as he did—and some days they brought in as much as five roubles. Vasha, too, brought in a little bit, breeding pigeons and selling them to fanciers. Often he'd be up on the roof, swinging a brush and whistling as the birds soared high into the sky. That wasn't enough for him, though, he wanted them higher yet. He trapped finches, starlings . . . made cages. . . .

"Not much in that, you'd think. Little things. But consider. Altogether, out of little things of that sort, he'd bring in ten roubles a month. . . .

"Well, as the months went by, the old woman lost the use of her legs and had to stay in bed. A house with no one to look after it, that's like a man without eyes, so she made up her mind to find a wife for Vasha. They called in a matchmaker, there was a lot of women's talk, and Vasha went off to see prospective brides. He picked Mashenka at the widow Samakval's. Without much reflection they blessed each other and so on and within a week the thing was all over. . . .

"The girl was young, just seventeen, neat and slender, with a fair-skinned pretty face, and well bred too; and with quite a nice dowry, five hundred roubles, a cow . . . a bed . . .

"Well, some three days after the wedding," Matvei went on, "the old woman, as if she'd expected it, went off to the heaven where there's no pain or suffering. The young couple prayed and started life together. Things went well too for the first six months until they'd further cause for grief. Troubles never come singly, do they?

"Vasha was summoned to the recruiting office where they draw lots for the call-up. They wanted him for a soldier and took him off, poor chap, no exemption granted. They shaved his head and sent him to Poland. That sort of thing is in the hands of God, what can a man do? Vasha didn't make much fuss as he said goodbye to her, but when he glanced over for the last time at the loft where the pigeons were, he burst into tears. It was pitiful to see.

"At first Mashenka's mother came to stay in case it was dull for her but after Kouska was born she went off to Oboyan to her

138

other married daughter and Mashenka was left alone with the child.

"Five draymen, rough and hard-drinking, horses, the dray-carts, the fence falling down or soot catching fire in the chimney ... it's more than a woman can cope with, so she began to turn to me, her neighbour, with her troubles. Well, you know how it is. You do your best to help, give advice and so on; and then you're dropping in for a cup of tea and a chat. I was a young fellow with plenty of ideas, eager to discuss every subject there is and she was well-educated and well-bred. She dressed well, too, and strolled under a parasol in the summer. . . .

"I used to talk to her about religion and politics and she was flattered, gave me tea and jam. . . .

"Well, to cut a long story short, I tell you, sir, in less than a year I was tempted by that wicked spirit, mankind's old enemy, the devil. I began to realise that whenever I didn't visit her I was restless, sick at heart and bored. I thought up every excuse to go to her. 'Time to put the window frames in for the winter,' I'd say and laze about all one day on the job, and still manage to leave two over for the next. Or it was, 'We'll have to count the pigeons in case there are any missing.' Always something.

"I used to talk to her a lot over the fence and in the end, to shorten the way, I made a wicket gate in it. . . .

"Females bring a lot of wickedness into this world, yes, all sorts of evil. Not only sinners like you and me but even saints can be led astray. Mashenka didn't in the least discourage me. Instead of controlling herself and keeping faith with her man, she took a fancy to me. . . .

"I noticed she was sick at heart and bored too, couldn't keep away from the fence and was always peeping through the gaps into my yard. My head began to spin with frenzied thoughts . . .

"Then one Thursday—it was in Holy Week—as I was going very early to the market, just after it was light, I passed close by her gate and, the devil prompting me, glanced in—she had a lattice at the top of it—and there she was, up already, in the middle of the yard, feeding the ducks. . . .

"I couldn't help myself. I called out. She came and looked

at me through the lattice, her little face white, her eyes sleepy and tender. . . .

"She attracted me so I began to compliment her as if we weren't meeting casually at a gate but I were there to pay my respects on her birthday; and she blushed, smiling at me and looking straight into my eyes without a flicker or a blink. . . .

"I lost my wits and told her how much I loved her.

"She opened the gate and I went in . . . and from that morning we lived as man and wife. . . ."

Aleshka the hunchback came into the yard from the road and hurried, panting, without a glance at anyone, into the house. A minute later he came out again with a concertina; jingling coppers in his pocket and crunching sunflower seeds, he ran through the gate.

"Who's that you have there?" asked Matvei Savitch.

"My son, Alexei," answered Doudya. "Up to his tricks again, the lazy rascal. God's burdened him with that hump so we're not too strict with him."

"Always playing with the lads, larking about," sighed Afanasevna. "We had him married before Shrovetide. We thought he'd be better then, but I reckon he's even worse. . . ."

"Yes, it's done no good," said Doudya. "Only pleasured someone else's lass for nothing."

A song, impressive and sad, swelled up from somewhere behind the church and everyone went quiet, listening. But they couldn't make out the words, only distinguish voices, two tenors and a bass. . . .

Two of the singers broke off quite suddenly in hoots of laughter but the other, a tenor voice, sang on and on, rising to such a pitch that everyone involuntarily looked up as if the voice were soaring there.

Barbara came out of the house and, shielding her eyes as if from the sun, peered across at the church.

"The priest's sons and the teacher," she said.

Again all three sang together. Matvei Savitch sighed and went on with his story:

"Well, that's how it was, sir. Then, after a couple of years we got a letter from Vasha in Warsaw. He said he was being sent home for convalescence. By that time I'd rid myself of my infatuation, and an excellent bride was being offered to me, but I'd seen no way of breaking with Mashenka. I'd resolved day after day to put it to her but how could I without provoking a flood of hysterical tears?

"Vasha's letter gave me my opportunity. We read it side by side and she went white as a sheet. I said: 'Oh, thank God, that means you can be a wife again!'

" 'No, I won't live with him,' she replied.

" 'He's your husband after all,' I said.

" 'That's so easy to say . . . but I never loved him. They forced me to him against my will. My mother made me.'

" 'Now, now,' I said. 'You can't get out of it like that, you little idiot. Did you stand with him there in the church or didn't you?'

" 'Of course I did. But it's you I love and I'll stay with you till I die. . . . Let them mock me if they like. I don't care.'

" 'Mashenka,' I said, 'you're a Christian. You've read the Scriptures. What do they say?' "

"A wife is given in marriage to her husband," said Doudya, "and must cleave to him."

"Yes, a husband and wife are one flesh," said Matvei Savitch. "I told her that. 'We've sinned together, you and I,' I said, 'and it's enough. We must obey our consciences and fear God. Let's confess to Vasha what we've done. He's a quiet man and shy: he won't beat you. And anyway, it's surely better to be punished by a lawful husband than to writhe in anguish on the Day of Judgement.'

"But the woman wouldn't listen. She'd set her mind against it. 'I love *you!*' That's all she'd say.

"Vasha came back on the Saturday before Trinity, early in the morning. I saw it all from the fence. He ran into the house but was out again a minute later with Kouska in his arms, laughing and crying. He kissed Kouska and then stared at the pigeons in

141

the hay. It gave him quite a pang to put the baby down but he wanted to go to those birds. He was a sensitive chap, of rather deep feeling.

"The day passed quietly without any fuss. But when the bells rang for evening service, I suddenly thought: 'Tomorrow's Trinity Sunday, why aren't they decking the gate and fence with green?' Something was wrong, so I went over.

"Vasha was sitting on the floor, rolling his eyes like a drunkard, tears wet on his cheeks, his hands all trembling. He'd pulled out rolls, cakes, sweetmeats and whatnot and scattered them all over the floor. Kouska—he must have been three by then—was crawling beside him, guzzling cakes, and Mashenka stood pale and trembling at the stove, muttering: 'I'm not your wife. I won't live with you.' A lot of nonsense!

"I went down on my knees to Vasha and said:

"'We have sinned against you, Vasily Maximitch. Please forgive us in the name of Christ.'

"Then I stood up and said to Mashenka:

"'Maria Semonovna, now you must wash the feet of Vasily Maximitch and drink the cup of repentance and be to him always a loyal, obedient wife. And I want you to pray to God for me too, that in His mercy he may forgive my sin.'

"I was as if inspired by the Holy Ghost. I spoke so feelingly that I too shed tears.

"Two days later Vasha came to see me.

"'I forgive you, Matyusha,' he said. 'And my wife, may God be with you both! She was a soldier's wife after all, left too long at home, it's the way young women are, it's hard for them to control their natures. She's not the first, no, nor the last. All I ask is that you live as if there'd been nothing at all between you. I myself won't say a word about it. I'll just try to please her in every way so that she comes to love me again.'

"He gave me his hand, we drank tea together and he went away contented. I was happy that things had turned out so well and thanked God for it. But Vasha was hardly out of the house before Mashenka came. What misery then! Flinging her arms round my neck, weeping, praying:

" 'For God's sake don't turn me away! I can't live without you!' "

"The bitch!" sighed Doudya.

"I shouted at her, stamped my foot, pushed her out and locked the door.
" 'Go back to your husband,' I said. 'Don't put me to shame before my neighbours, have fear of God!'
"But every day it was the same story. . . .
"Then one morning when I was cleaning a bridle near the stable, I saw her running through the little gate into my yard, barefoot, in only a petticoat, coming straight at me. She snatched the bridle, smearing herself with the pitch, trembling and weeping:
" 'I can't live with him. He's horrible. I haven't the strength. . . . If you don't love me, it's best you kill me.'
"I lost my temper and struck her twice with the bridle; and then Vasha came running through the gate shouting wildly: 'Don't beat her! Don't beat her!' But he went for her himself, laying on like a madman, punching her with all his strength; then he flung her to the ground and kicked her. I tried to protect her but he snatched up some reins and thrashed her with those. And all the time he was whinnying like a colt: 'Heigh! Heigh! Heigh!' "

"I'd take the reins to you, that's what I'd do . . ." muttered Barbara, going out. "Murdering our sister, curse you! . . ."
"Shut your mouth, you!" shouted Doudya. "You cow!"

" 'Heigh! Heigh! Heigh!' " went on Matvei Savitch. "Well, a drayman ran in from next door and I shouted for one of my workmen and between us we got Mashenka away from him and carried her home. The shame of it! That evening I went to see her. She lay in bed so wrapped in bandages she was all muffled up, only her nose and eyes to be seen, staring up at the ceiling.
" 'Hello, Maria Semonovna, how are you?'

143

"Silence!

"Vasha sat in the next room, clutching his head and crying out: 'What a swine I am! I've ruined my life. Let me die, oh God!'

"I sat by Mashenka for half an hour and admonished her. I tried to frighten her a little. The innocent on this earth, I said, go to heaven, but if you're like this, you'll go to the fiery furnace with the harlots. Don't disobey your husband. Go and kneel for his forgiveness.

"She didn't say a word, didn't even blink her eye. I might have been talking to a statue.

"Next day Vasha fell ill: of a fever rather like cholera. And in the evening they told me he was dead. Mashenka didn't go to his funeral, she didn't want people to see her bruised and shameful face. And soon the rumour was in all the drawing rooms that Vasha didn't die a natural death, she killed him. It reached the authorities. They exhumed Vasha and found arsenic in his stomach: it was clear he'd taken it with his food.

"The Police came for Mashenka and took her and Kouska, poor innocent lad, to prison. The woman had gone too far, now God was punishing her. . . .

"After eight months she came to trial. She sat there in the dock, I remember, in a white kerchief and grey smock, so thin and pale and with such piercing eyes. It was pitiful to see. A soldier with a rifle stood behind her. She didn't confess. A section of the court maintained she poisoned her husband, another argued that he killed himself in grief.

"I was called as a witness. I answered all questions honestly according to my conscience, telling of her sin, the plain fact that she didn't love her husband, that by nature she was . . .

"The court met in the morning and it was evening before they brought in their verdict: hard labour in Siberia for thirteen years. For some three months, though, after the verdict Mashenka was in our local prison. I went to see her, in charity taking her tea and sugar. But as soon as she saw me, she trembled from top to toe, wrung her hands and shouted, 'Go away, go away!' And she clutched Kouska to her, as if afraid I'd take him.

144

" 'Look what you've brought yourself to, Mashenka,' I said. 'Oh, Masha, Masha, poor soul! You didn't listen when I showed you the way of reason and now you weep for it. You have only yourself to blame.'

"I showed her the error of her ways but it was just 'Go away, go away!' and clutching Kouska close to the wall and trembling.

"When they took her to the provincial capital, I went to see her off at the station and for the good of my soul thrust a little money into her bundle. But she didn't reach Siberia. She caught a fever in the central prison and died there."

"A bitch must die a bitch's death," said Doudya.

"They brought Kouska home. After deep thought I decided to bring him up. What else could I do? The child of a criminal, yes, but a human soul and a baptised Christian. . . . An object of compassion. I'll make him my clerk and if I've no children I'll see he's a merchant. He comes with me wherever I go to learn the business."

While Matvei Savitch was speaking, Kouska sat on a stone near the gate, hands clutched behind his head, staring up into the sky: at that distance in the dark he looked like a tree stump.

"Kouska, go to bed!" shouted Matvei Savitch.

"Yes, it's time," said Doudya, getting up. He made a noisy yawn and went on: "All for going their own way, disobedient, and that's how things turn out."

The moon was gliding over the courtyard, going swiftly in one direction, the clouds below it in another. The clouds were disappearing but the moon could still be seen high up. Matvei Savitch said a prayer towards the church and then, bidding goodnight, lay on the ground near the cart. Kouska prayed too, then wrapped himself in his overcoat and lay in the cart. To get comfortable he made a little pit in the hay and curled up till his elbows looked like his knees. Doudya could be seen in a downstairs room lighting a candle, putting on his spectacles and stand-

145

ing in a corner with a book. For a long time he read and nodded.

The travellers fell asleep. Afanasevna and Sophia came to the cart and looked at Kouska.

"The orphan's asleep," said the old lady. "So thin and skinny, he's all bone. His own mother's gone, who's to see he's fed properly?"

"My little Grishka must be two years older," said Sophia. "He has to live locked up in the factory away from his mother. I wouldn't be surprised if the master doesn't beat him. When I saw this chap tonight, I remembered Grishka and my blood ran cold."

There was a minute's silence.

"Perhaps he doesn't remember his mother," said the old lady. "How could he?"

Tears ran from Sophia's eye.

"The little chap's all curled up," she said, sobbing and laughing with pity and affection. "Poor old orphan!"

Kouska started and opened his eyes. He saw in front of him an ugly, wrinkled tear-stained face, another beside it, a toothless old woman's with sharp chin and hooked nose, and above them a sky as far as the eye could see with sliding clouds and moon—and he cried out in terror. Sophia cried out too. Echoes answered both, bringing a hovering disquiet to the sultry air. A watchman knocked with his stick in a neighbouring yard and a dog barked.

Matvei Savitch muttered something in his sleep and turned over.

Later in the night when Doudya was also asleep, the old lady too and the watchman, Sophia went out of the gate and sat on a bench. She felt stifled and her head ached from crying. The road was broad and long, more than a mile in each direction further than you could see. The moon had passed over the courtyard and was above the church. One side of the road was washed in moonlight, the other deep in dark. The long shadows of the poplars and the starling-cotes stretched over and the church cast forbidding gloom on the gate and half of Doudya's house.

It was very quiet, no one about. The faintest music came

146

now and then from far along the street—Aleshka, probably, with his concertina.

In the shadow of the church fence something moved. Impossible to tell if it were a man or a cow, or neither, perhaps a huge bird rustling among the leaves. Then a figure emerged from the dark, stopped, said something in a man's voice, then disappeared into a lane beside the church. A little later a second figure appeared, about three yards away. It had come from the church and was making for the gate. At the sight of Sophia on the bench it stopped.

"Barbara, is that you?" asked Sophia.

"What if it is?"

Yes, it was Barbara. She stood a moment, then went to the bench and sat down.

"Where've you been?"

Barbara didn't answer.

"Carry on like this, my girl," said Sophia, "and you'll come to grief. Didn't you hear how they kicked Mashenka and thrashed her with reins? Look out, or they'll do that to you."

"Let them!"

Barbara giggled against her kerchief and whispered: "I've had a fine time with the priest's son."

"You're kidding."

"No, I swear it, by God."

"It's a sin," whispered Sophia.

"Let it be. What's there to be sorry about? All right, it's a sin, a real sin, but better be struck by lightning than put up with this life here. I'm young and strong and my husband's a horrible twisted hunchback, worse than that cursed Doudya! When I was a girl, I'd little enough bread and ran barefoot, and Alexei's money tempted me to get away from that misery. And I gave in despite myself, yes, I was trapped like a fish in a basket but I'd rather sleep with a snake than with that lousy Alexei. And what about you and your life? I couldn't face it. Your Fedor sent you away here to his father and he's taken another in your place. And they've dragged your son to the factory, you couldn't stop them. You work like a carthorse and never get a kind word. Better live out our suffering lives as tarts, eh, pick up fifty kopeks from a priest's son, better go begging, or put our heads on the block, eh . . . ?"

"It's a sin," whispered Sophia again.

"Let it be!"

Somewhere from behind the church the same three voices sang mournfully again together, two tenors and a bass; and it was still impossible to distinguish a word.

"Ah, the night birds!" giggled Barbara.

And she began to whisper what a time she had at nights with the priest's son, the things he told her, what his pals were like, and how she'd done the same thing with travelling officials and merchants.

The sad song brought a longing for freedom. Sophia began to chuckle—it was as if she were a sinner too and it was frightening and yet so sweet to listen—she was envious and sorry for herself that she didn't sin like that when she was young and pretty.

From the churchyard they heard the stroke of midnight.

"Time to go to bed," said Sophia, standing up, "or Doudya might catch us."

They moved silently into the courtyard.

"I went away and didn't hear him tell what happened to Mashenka," said Barbara, settling under the window.

"She died in prison. She'd poisoned her husband."

Barbara lay beside Sophia, brooded a little, then whispered: "I'd do for that Aleshka and not be sorry."

"That's nonsense you're talking, God help you!"

When Sophia was dropping off, Barbara snuggled close to her and muttered in her ear:

"Let's do for both Aleshka and Doudya!"

Sophia winced but did not speak, then opened her eyes and stared for a long time at the sky, quite motionless.

"People would find out," she said.

"They wouldn't. Doudya's old, it's time for him to go, and Aleshka, why, they'd say he died of drink."

148

"It's terrible. God would punish us!"

"Let Him!"

Neither spoke, brooding in the silence.

"It's cold," said Sophia, starting to tremble from top to toe. "It must be nearly morning. Are you asleep?"

"No. . . . Don't you listen to me, love," whispered Barbara. "I hate them so, curse them, till I don't know what I'm saying. Go to sleep. It'll be daybreak directly. Sleep."

They remained silent, at their ease, and soon fell asleep.

The old lady was the first to stir. She woke Sophia and both went into the shed to milk the cows. Aleshka the hunchback came home, drunk as a lord, without his concertina, his chest and knees thick with dust and chaff. He must have fallen somewhere. He staggered under the shed and without pulling off his clothes rolled into a sledge and began to snore.

The crosses on the church glinted in the rising sun's bright rays, then the windows, and the shadows of the trees and the well stretched over the dewy grass; Matvei Savitch got up and fussed about.

"Kouska, up with you!" he shouted. "Time to harness. Look lively!"

The morning bustle started. A young Jewess in a brown frilled skirt led in a horse for water. The well's pulley creaked mournfully, the bucket rattled . . .

Kouska, sluggish with sleep and wet with dew, sat up in the cart and lazily pulled on his overcoat. He listened to the well water dripping from the bucket and shivered with cold.

"Auntie," shouted Matvei Savitch to Sophia, "tell my lad to get a move on and harness the horses!"

At the same time Doudya shouted from the window:

"Sophia, get a copek from the Jewess for the water. Making a habit of it, the scraggy things!"

Sheep ran bleating up and down the road. Women shouted for the shepherd but he was playing on a pipe. He cracked his whip and answered them in a deep husky voice. Three sheep ran into the yard and, not finding a way out, butted the fence. The din woke Barbara who bundled up her bed and took it into the house.

"Can't you drive the sheep out?" the old lady shouted at her. "Too posh, eh?"

"I like that," muttered Barbara, as she went in. "Think I'll work for slavedrivers like you?"

They oiled the carriage wheels and harnessed the horses. Doudya came out of the house with his account book and sat on the step to calculate how much the travellers owed for their lodging and the feeding and watering of their horses.

"You're asking a lot for the oats, old man," said Matvei Savitch.

"You can always refuse if it's too dear. Up to you, merchant, we don't make you buy."

When the travellers were getting in the cart, there was a minute's delay: Kouska's cap was missing.

"Where'd you put it, stupid pig?" shouted Matvei Savitch. "Where is it?"

Kouska's face wrinkled up in fear. He rushed round the cart and, not finding it, ran to the gate and then under the shed. Sophia and the old lady helped him to look.

"I'll box your years, you dirty little rascal!" shouted Matvei Savitch.

The cap was found at the bottom of the cart. Kouska knocked the hay from it with his sleeve and put it on.

Matvei Savitch crossed himself, the driver tugged at the reins and the cart rumbled forward and out of the yard.

After the Theatre
1892

WHEN SHE CAME back with Mummy from the theatre where they saw *Eugene Onegin*, Nadia Zelenin went to her room, hurriedly thrust off her dress, let down her hair and in only a petticoat and white blouse sat quicker still to the table to write a letter like Tatiana's.

"I love you," she wrote down, "but you do not love me, do not love me!"

She wrote it down and began to laugh.

She was only sixteen and so far was in love with no one. She knew that Gorni, the officer, and Gruzdev, the student, were in love with her but now, after the opera, she wished to feel doubt of their love. To be unloved and unhappy—how interesting that was! When one loves greatly but the other is indifferent, there is something beautiful in that, affecting and poetic. Onegin is interesting because he is not in love at all and Tatiana fascinating because she loves so much, but if they loved each other just the same and both were happy, then, very likely, they would seem boring.

"Do stop declaring that you love me," Nadia went on, thinking of Gorni. "I cannot believe you. You are very clever, well-educated and earnest, you have immense talent and perhaps a brilliant future awaits you, while I am a dull girl of no account and you know perfectly well I would only be a hindrance in your life. True, you were attracted by me and thought that in me

151

you had found your ideal but it was a mistake and now you ask yourself in despair: 'What did I meet this girl for?' And only your kind nature prevents you from admitting that to yourself."

Nadia felt sorry for herself, began to cry and went on:

"It is hard for me to leave Mummy and my brother or I would put on a nun's dress and go away wherever my eyes may lead me. And you would be free and come to love another. Ah, if only I were dead!"

Through tears she could not make out what she wrote; and on the table, floor and ceiling little rainbows flickered as if she were looking through a prism. She could not write and leaned back in the chair and began to think about Gorni.

My God, how interesting men were, how fascinating! She remembered what a lovely look there was on Gorni's face, fawning, guilty and gentle, when they argued about music and what an effort he exerted to keep the sound of passion from his voice. In a society where indifference and chill arrogance are counted signs of breeding and of noble manners men have to hide their passion. And hide it he did, but unsuccessfully and everybody clearly knew that he loved music passionately. Endless debate about music and the bold assertions of the ignorant always put him under strain and he was apprehensive, shy and reticent. He played magnificently like a professional pianist and, had he not become an officer, would indeed be a famous musician.

The tears dried about her eyes. She remembered that Gorni declared his love for her at a symphony concert and then again downstairs near the cloak room, with draughts blowing all over the place.

"I'm very glad," she wrote, "that at last you've been introduced to Grusdev. He is a very clever man and you are certain to like him. He was with us yesterday and stayed till two o'clock. We were all delighted and I was sorry you hadn't come. He said a lot of wonderful things."

Nadia laid her arms on the table and rested her head on them, her hair covering the letter. She remembered that Grusdev was in love with her as well and had as much right to a letter as

152

Gorni. For that matter wouldn't it be better to write to Grusdev?

Quite without reason joy stirred in her breast: small at first, it rolled there like a rubber ball, then grew broader and larger and gushed like a wave. She forgot Gorni and Grusdev now, her thoughts became confused and her joy grew and grew, spreading from her breasts into her arms and legs, and it seemed as if a light, fresh breeze puffed about her head, ruffling her hair. Her shoulders trembled with a quiet laughter, and the table trembled too, and the glass round the lamp; and tears spattered on the letter from her eyes. It wasn't in her power to stop this laughter and to show herself she wasn't laughing without reason, she hastened to think of something funny.

"What a funny poodle!" she said, feeling as if the laughter would choke her. "What a funny poodle!"

She remembered how after tea the previous evening Grusdev had played with Maxim, the poodle, and then told a story about a very clever poodle who chased a raven in a yard and the raven looked back at him and said:

"Oh, you rascal!"

Not knowing he was up against a learned raven, the poodle was terribly bewildered, retreated in confusion, then began to bark.

"No, I'd better be in love with Grusdev!" Nadia decided and tore up the letter.

She began to think of the student and of his love and of her own love but then it seemed her thoughts ran off in all directions and she thought about everything: Mummy, the street, her pencil, the piano.

She brooded with delight and found everything splendid and wonderful, and her joy let her know that this was still not all, that in a little time it would be better still. Spring soon, summer, going to Gorbiki with Mummy, Gorni coming on leave and he would walk with her in the garden and make love. And Grusdev coming too. He would play croquet with her and skittles, tell her funny and astonishing things. A passionate longing came upon her for the garden, for darkness, clear sky and stars. Again her shoulders trembled with laughter and it seemed there was a scent of wormwood in the room and a twig tapped at the window.

She went to her bed and sat down; and not knowing what to do with the great joy that oppressed her, looked at the holy image hanging at her bedhead and said:

"God! God! God!"

Anna round the Neck
1895

AFTER THE WEDDING there was not even a light snack: the couple merely drank a glass, changed and rode to the station. Instead of a lively bridal ball and supper, instead of music and dancing, they journeyed to a shrine of pilgrimage two hundred versts away.

Many approved, saying that Modest Alexeitch was, after all, an important civil servant and no longer young so that a noisy wedding party wouldn't be quite the thing and music, too—when a public servant of fifty-two is marrying a girl of scarcely eighteen —is apt to pall. Modest Alexeitch, they added, like a man of principle, had especially arranged the visit to the shrine to show his young wife that morality and religion came first with him in marriage.

They were seen off. On the platform a crowd of colleagues and relatives held up their glasses, waiting to shout "Hurrah!" as the train moved; and Piotr Leontitch, her father, in top hat and teacher's uniform, drunk already and already very pale, kept stretching up towards the window with his glass and pleading:

"Aniuta! Anna! Anna! Just a word!"

Anna leaned out to him and he whispered something, oozing about her a smell of stale wine as he blew in her ear—impossible to understand a thing—and making the sign of the cross over her face, her breasts, her arms; he shivered as he gasped and tears gleamed in his eyes. And Anna's schoolboy brothers, Petya and Andrusha, tugged at his coat tails and whispered nervously:

"Father, that will do. . . . Father, there's no need . . ."

When the train started, Anna watched as her father ran a little way after the carriage, stumbling and spilling his wine, and saw how kind and pitiful and guilty his face looked.

"Hurra . . a . . ah!" he shouted.

The couple were at last alone. Modest Alexeitch looked around the compartment, spread his things on the racks and sat smiling opposite his young wife. He was a civil servant of average height, stout, pudgy and well-fed, with long side-whiskers and no moustache, his curving, clean-shaven, sharp-edged chin looking like a heel. His most characteristic feature was the bare, fresh-shaven space where no moustache was, spreading to fat cheeks quivering like jelly. He was sedate, slow of movement and soft of manner.

"I can't help calling to mind a certain event," he said, smiling. "Five years ago, when Kosorotov was awarded the order of Saint Anna, second class, and went to express his thanks, His Excellency said these words: 'This means you have three Annas now: one in your lapel and two around your neck.' Kosorotov's wife, I ought to say, had just come back to him, a flighty and peevish woman, and her name was Anna. I hope that, when I am awarded the order of Saint Anna, second class, His Excellency will not have occasion to say the same thing to me."

He smiled with his little eyes. And she smiled too, disturbed by the thought that at any moment this man could kiss her with his plump, damp lips and that she had no right to refuse him. The soft movements of his fat body frightened her: she was terrified and disgusted.

He stood, unhurriedly took off the order from his neck, then his coat and waistcoat and put on a dressing gown.

"There we are," he said, as he sat down beside her.

She remembered the agony of the ceremony, her feeling that the priest, the guests and everyone in the church were looking at her with pity: why was such a darling of a girl marrying this middle-aged, dull man? Only that morning she'd been delighted how everything had been arranged but at the wedding itself and now in the railway carriage she felt guilty, cheated and ridiculous. Yes, she'd married a rich man but she'd no money at all, her wedding dress was bought on credit and when her father and brothers saw her off, she could tell from their faces they hadn't a penny. Would they even have anything to eat that night? Or tomorrow? For some reason she imagined her father and the boys sitting hungry without her, feeling just the misery they felt the evening of her mother's funeral.

"Oh, how miserable I am!" she thought. "Why am I so miserable?"

A sedate man, awkward now because he was unaccustomed to women, Modest Alexeitch touched her at the waist and patted her shoulder and she went on thinking about money and her mother and her mother's death. Her father, Piotr Leontitch, who taught drawing and handwriting in a high school, took to drink when her mother died and then penury came upon them, the boys with neither boots nor galoshes, her father taken to court, the receiver coming to the house and making an inventory of the furniture. The shame of it! Anna had to look after her drunken father, darn her brothers' stockings, do the shopping and when people complimented her on her youthful beauty and graceful manners, she felt they were all noticing her cheap hat and the inked-over holes in her shoes. And at nights she cried, dreading all the time that soon, very soon, they'd turn her father out of his school for incompetence, that he wouldn't be able to take it and die like her mother. But then ladies they knew had fussed about looking for a suitable man for her and very quickly found this Modest Alexeitch who was neither young nor handsome but had money: a hundred thousand in the bank and a family estate that was rented to a tenant. He was a man of principle, in good standing with His Excellency; a mere nothing for him, they told Anna, to send a note to the school governors or even to the Education Officer to stop them from dismissing her father.

As she recalled these things she suddenly heard music and the sound of voices through the window. The train had stopped at a station. Beyond the platform was a crowd and an accordion was playing and a cheap squeaky violin and further, from beyond high birch trees and poplars and villas too, lit by moonlight, came the noise of a military band. There must be a dance on the estate. Summer visitors and townsfolk who travelled out there in good weather for the fresh country air were walking up and down the platform. Among them was Artinov who was very rich and owned every one of the villas, a tall, fat, dark man with bulging eyes and a face like an Armenian: oddly dressed, his shirt open on his chest, his boots high and with spurs, and a dark cloak hanging down from his shoulders to drag over the ground like a train. Two boarhounds followed him, their sharp snouts to the ground.

There was a gleam of tears still in Anna's eyes but her thoughts were no longer of her mother and money and her marriage: laughing gaily, she shook hands with students and officers whom she knew, saying quickly:

"Good evening. How do you do?"

She went out on the platform in the moonlight and stood so that everyone could see her magnificent new dress and hat.

"Why are we stopping here?" she asked.

"It's a junction," she was told. "We're waiting for the mail train to come through."

Noticing Artinov look at her, she crinkled up her eyes coquettishly and began to chat noisily in French; and because her own voice sounded so pleasant and there was music, and moonlight reflected in a pool, and because Artinov, well-known for a rogue and a Don Juan, looked at her with avid curiosity, and everyone was gay, she felt suddenly happy; and when the train was starting and the officers she knew saluted her, she found herself humming the polka played by the military band somewhere beyond the trees, and got into her compartment feeling as if it had been made certain there at the station that she would really be happy in spite of everything.

The couple spent two days at the monastery, then returned

to town and lived in a rent-free flat for civil servants. When
Modest Alexeitch was at the office, Anna played the piano or
lay on the couch reading novels or turning the pages of fashion
magazines. Modest Alexeitch ate big meals at dinner and talked
of politics, appointments, transfers and promotions; saying that
hard work was needed, family life was not a pleasure but a duty,
to save copecks was to save roubles, and that he put religion and
morality above all else in this world. Clasping his knife in his
fist like a sword, he said:

"Every man should have his duties!"

Listening, Anna became agitated and couldn't eat and usually
left the table hungry. After dinner her husband lay down and
snored and she would go out to see her people. Her father and
brothers looked at her strangely as if just before she came
in they had been blaming her for marrying for money a dull bore
of a man she didn't love. Her rustling skirts, her bracelets and
her ladylike ways embarrassed and offended them, they were ill
at ease when she was there and didn't know what to talk about
with her; but they loved her for all that as they always did and
were still not used to having dinner without her. She sat and
ate with them their porridge and their cabbage soup and their
potatoes fried in smelly mutton fat. Piotr Leontitch, his hand
trembling, filled a glass from a decanter and drank it down
greedily, disgustingly, and then another and another. . . . Petya
and Andrusha, thin and pale, with big eyes, took away the
decanter, mumbling in embarrassment:

"That will do, Father. . . . Father, that's enough. . . ."

Anna too was uneasy and begged him not to drink any more
but he suddenly flushed with anger and beat the table with
his fists.

"I let nobody order me about!" he shouted. "Kids! Slip of a
girl! I'll chuck the three of you out!"

His voice, though, had a weak sound, a kindliness, and no one
was afraid of him.

Usually after dinner he dressed up: pale, a cut on his chin
from shaving, stretching his skinny neck, he'd stand a full half

hour in front of the mirror, preening, brushing his hair, twisting his black moustache, sprinkling scent, and setting his tie in a bow; then he'd put on his top hat and gloves and go off to do his private coaching. Or if it were a holiday he'd stay at home and paint or play the wheezy, snarling harmonium, trying to squeeze some pure concordant notes from it and sing, or, if he couldn't, shout at the boys:

"Scoundrels! Villains! You've ruined this instrument!"

In the evening Anna's husband played cards with his colleagues in the civil servants' flats. Their wives came too, ugly women dressed without taste, coarse as cooks, and indulged, there in the flat, in gossip as vulgar and graceless as themselves. Occasionally Modest Alexeitch would take Anna to the theatre. Between the acts he wouldn't let her move a step away from him, walking arm in arm with her through the corridors and foyer. As he bowed to someone, he whispered there and then to Anna: "A civil councillor . . . Received by His Excellency . . ." or: "A man of means . . . Owns his own house . . ." When they came to the buffet, Anna longed for something sweet—she loved chocolate and apple tart—but she'd no money and was ashamed to ask her husband. He would pick up a pear, pinch it with his fingers and ask with doubting voice:

"How much?"

"Twenty-five copecks!"

"I ask you!" he would say and put it back; but because it looked bad to leave the buffet without buying anything he would ask for seltzer water and drink the whole bottle himself till tears came in his eyes. She hated him then.

Suddenly his face would flush red and he'd mutter quickly:

"Bow to that old lady!"

"But I don't know her."

"Never mind. It's the wife of the treasury director! Go on, bow, I tell you!" he snapped grumpily. "Your head won't drop off!"

She did bow and of course her head didn't drop off but it was torture all the same. She did everything he wanted and hated herself for being taken in like the stupidest of idiots. She had only

160

married him for his money and yet she had less now than before her marriage. Before, her father would sometimes give her twenty copecks— now she didn't even get a half! She couldn't sneak his money or ask him for it, she was in fear and trembling. It was as if in her mind she had feared that man from long ago. From her childhood even, when the high school Headmaster seemed a terrible and awe-inspiring force poised like a storm cloud or a steam engine to crush her to pieces. And another force like that which all the family talked about and were afraid of, was His Excellency; and there were a dozen or so others too, like the teachers, smooth-lipped, stern and relentless; and now, last of all, Modest Alexeitch, the man of principle, whose face even looked like the Headmaster's.

In Anna's imagination they all blended into one thing, a sort of immense and terrible white bear that loomed threatening over weak and erring people like her father. And she was afraid to say a word in opposition to her husband and made herself smile and ape pleasure under coarse embraces and degrading fondling that stirred her with horror.

Just once her father dared to ask him for a loan of fifty roubles to pay off a very pressing debt, and it had been agony!

"Very well, I will give it you," said Modest Alexeitch, thinking a moment. "But I warn you I will not help you any more until you give up drink. For a man in the civil service it's a disgusting weakness. I cannot but remind you of the well-known fact that such a passion has ruined many talented men who might otherwise quite possibly have risen with sobriety to positions of importance."

The long-winded phrases went on and on: "in so far as . . . ," "in consequence of which . . . ," "in view of what has been stated . . ."; and poor Piotr Leontitch was in an agony of embarrassment and longing for a drink.

And if the boys came to visit Anna, usually with their boots torn and their trousers shabby, they too had to listen to a sermon.

"Every man should have his duties!" he told them.

He gave no money: but he gave presents of bracelets, rings

and brooches to Anna, saying that such things came in useful in hard times. And often he unlocked her drawer and searched most thoroughly to see that all were there.

2

In the meantime winter came on; and long before Christmas the local paper announced the usual winter ball on December 29th in the Hall of Nobles. Every evening after cards Modest Alexeitch kept whispering excitedly to the civil servants' wives and glancing anxiously at Anna and then walked to and fro, pre-occupied, a long time; and finally, late one evening, he stopped in front of her and said:

"You have to buy a party dress. Do you understand? Only please talk to Maria Grigorievna and Natalia Kuzminishna about it."

And he gave her a hundred roubles. She took it; but she consulted no one when she ordered the dress, speaking about it only to her father and trying to imagine how her mother would have dressed for a ball. She had always put on the latest fashion and fussed over Anna too, dressing her daintily like a doll and teaching her to speak French and dance a splendid mazurka. (For five years before her marriage she had been a governess.) Anna, like her, could create a new dress from an old one, clean gloves with paraffin, get jewels on hire, and, like her too, could crinkle up her eyes, murmur, set herself in pretty posture, glow rapturously when needed and gaze mysteriously and sadly. From her father came her dark hair and eyes, her highly-strung nature and the way she kept on preening herself.

Half an hour before they left for the ball Modest Alexeitch came to her room, no frock coat on, to set his order about his neck at her looking glass; fascinated by her beauty and the sheen of her light and airy dress, he combed his whiskers conceitedly and said:

"So that's what my wife is like . . . that's what you're like!

"Aniuta!" he went on, his tone suddenly serious. "I've made

you happy, now you can make me happy too. I beg you, intro-
duce yourself to His Excellency's wife. Do, for God's sake! With
her help I may be promoted to senior registrar."

They went to the ball. There they were at the Hall of Nobles,
in the entrance where the porter was; then the foyer with cloak
room and fur coats, hurrying footmen and ladies in low dresses
screening themselves with fans from chill draughts; it smelled of
gas lamps and soldiers. As Anna, going up the staircase on her
husband's arm, heard music and saw herself, all of her, reflected
by a huge mirror in a mass of lights, a glow of joy lifted her
spirits and she felt the same anticipation of happiness as that
moonlit evening at the station.

She walked proudly, confidently, aware of herself for the
first time not as girl but as lady, assuming unconsciously the walk
and gesture of her mother. For the first time she felt rich and
free. Even her husband, there beside her, did not inhibit her
for, moving into the hall, she guessed instinctively that an old
husband by her side did not humiliate her; on the contrary, it
gave her the air of piquant mystery so fascinating to men.

The orchestra was playing and dancing had begun. Over-
whelmed, after the civil servant's flat, by lights, many colours,
music and noise, Anna looked all round the hall and thought,
"Oh, how wonderful!", recognizing at once in the throng people
she knew, people she had met at parties and picnics, officers,
teachers, lawyers, officials, landowners, His Excellency, Artinov,
and high-born ladies, dressed in the finest, very low-necked,
pretty and plain, there already at the stalls of the charity bazaar
to sell things for the poor.

A huge officer in epaulettes—she'd been introduced to him
once in Old Kiev Street when she was a schoolgirl and now
couldn't remember his name—rose up as if out of the ground
and asked her to waltz and she swung away from her husband,
feeling as though she were on a sailing ship in a strong storm and
he left far behind on the shore. She danced with passion,
fervently; a waltz, a polka, a quadrille, passed from one man's

arms to another's, dazed with music and noise, mixing Russian and French, murmuring, laughing, with no thought of her husband, no thought of anyone or anything. She was a great success with the men, it was obvious, couldn't be otherwise, and she went breathless with excitement, clutching convulsively at her fan and longing for a drink. Her father, Piotr Leontitch, in a rumpled frock coat smelling of petrol, came to her with a saucer of pink ice-cream.

"You're charming tonight," he said, gazing at her with great pleasure. "I've never felt so sorry that you rushed and got married. Why did you? I know you did it for our sake but . . ." With trembling hands he pulled out a wad of notes and said: "I got paid for my lessons today and I can give your husband what I owe him."

She put the saucer back in his hand and was snatched up by someone and swept away, glimpsing him across her partner's shoulder, gliding over the floor, slipping his arm around a lady and whirling her about the room.

"What a dear he is," she thought, "when he's sober!"

She danced a mazurka with the same huge officer; he stepped gravely, heavily, like a corpse in uniform, jerking his shoulders and chest, treading lazily—the dancing utterly against his inclination—but she fluttered about him, teasing him with her beauty, her deep bare neck, her eyes glowing fervently, her movements passionate, and he bcame more thoroughly indifferent, stretching his arms to her courteously like a king.

"Bravo! Bravo!" called the watching people.

But little by little the huge officer gave in; he became excited, very lively, and, fascinated by her, gave rein to his passion and danced light-footedly, youthfully and it was she now who jerked her shoulders and looked at him archly as if she were the queen and he the slave and it seemed to her then that all the people in the hall were watching them, thrilled and envying.

Scarcely had the huge officer managed to thank her for the dance when the people suddenly gave way about her, the men standing strangely straight, arms at their sides . . . and His

Excellency walked towards her in frock coat with two stars. Yes, His Excellency was walking definitely to her for he was staring steadily at her with a sugary smile and licking his lips as he always did at the sight of a good-looking woman.

"Enchanted, enchanted . . ." he began. "I'll have your husband sitting in the guard room for hiding from us till now such a charmer. I have a message for you from my wife," he went on, giving her his arm. "You must help us . . . H'm . . . We shall have to give you the prize for beauty . . . As in America . . . H'm . . . The Americans. . . . My wife is impatient to see you."

He led her to a middle-aged lady at a stall, the lower part of her face unusually large as if she had a big stone in her mouth.

"Help us," she murmured, sing-song through the nose. "All the pretty women are working for the charity bazaar, you're the only one gadding about. Why don't you help us?"

She went away and Anna took over her place by the teacups and the silver samovar; and at once a lively trade began. She asked no less than a rouble for each cup and made the huge officer drink three. Artinov, the rich man, came up to her, bulging-eyed, asthmatic, no longer in the strange costume in which she'd seen him in the summer at the station but in evening dress like all the others. Without taking his eyes from Anna he drank a glass of champagne and paid a hundred roubles and then a cup of tea and paid another hundred: silent all the time, his asthma troubling him . . .

Anna invited others to purchase and took their money, deeply convinced now that her smiles and glances couldn't fail to give them great pleasure. Indeed she realised she had been made for just this life, noisy, glittering and full of laughter, where there was music and dancing and male admirers; and her fear from long ago, her terror before a looming force threatening to crush her, seemed quite ridiculous. She was afraid of no one now and only regretted that her mother could not be there to delight at her success.

Piotr Leontitch, pale now but still steady on his legs, came to the stall and asked for a glass of brandy. She blushed, expecting him to say something improper (ashamed already of such a poor and undistinguished father) but he drank it down, peeled ten roubles from his wad of notes and went off rather pompously, not saying a word. A little later she saw him dancing with a partner in *le grand rond* but by then he was reeling about, yelling something, quite confusing his lady, and she remembered how three years ago he yelled and reeled like that at a ball and in the end a Policeman took him home and put him to bed and next day the Headmaster threatened to dismiss him. How unpleasant it was to remember that at this time!

When they put out the samovars in the stalls and the tired charity-workers handed over their takings to the middle-aged lady with a stone in her mouth, Artinov led Anna by the arm to the room where supper was provided for those who had worked at the charity bazaar. Twenty sat down, no more, but it was very noisy. His Excellency proposed a toast:

"It is fitting in this splendid dining-room to drink to the success of those other modest dining rooms in aid of which today's bazaar was organized."

A Brigadier General proposed a toast "to that force before which even artillery gives in," and they all clinked their glasses with the ladies. It was very, very gay.

As Anna was driven home it was already daylight and cooks were going to market. Happy, intoxicated, worn-out and full of new sensations, she took her clothes off, dropped into bed and there and then fell asleep.

Early in the afternoon the housemaid awoke her with the information that Mr. Artinov had come to visit her. She dressed quickly and went into the drawing room. Soon after Artinov His Excellency called, too, and thanked her for her work at the charity bazaar. With sugary smile and gulping lips he kissed her hand and asked to be allowed to call again and went away; and she stood in the middle of the drawing room, amazed, fascinated, quite unable to believe how her life had changed,

166

changed wonderfully and so quickly; and just as that moment her husband walked in, Modest Alexeitch . . . And he too stood before her with the same unctuous, sickly-sweet and toadying expression she used to see on his face when he was with powerful and well-known people; and with delight and anger and scorn, quite sure now of nothing more to fear from him, she said, accentuating each word:

"Off with you, you clot!"

From that time on Anna had no day to spare, was always at picnics, excursions and shows. Every day she came back in the early hours and lay down to sleep on the drawing room floor, telling everybody afterwards, quite touchingly, that she had slept under flowers. She needed a great deal of money but she didn't fear Modest Alexeitch anymore and took his as her own, not asking nor demanding, only sending him the bills or notes of this sort: "Give bearer 200 roubles" or "Required at once, 100 roubles."

At Easter Modest Alexeitch was awarded the order of Anna, second class. When he went to offer thanks, His Excellency laid his newspaper aside and settled himself more deeply in his chair.

"So now you have three Annas," he said, looking carefully at his white hands with pink nails. "One on your lapel and two round your neck."

Modest Alexeitch put two fingers to his lips to stop a noisy laugh and said:

"Now I'm only waiting for a little Vladimir to see the light. Dare I beg your Excellency to be his godfather."

He meant the order of Vladimir, fourth class and already imagined how he would recount to everyone his pun, so neat in its point and daring, and he wanted to say something equally neat but His Excellency, buried again in his newspaper, merely nodded . . .

And Anna went driving in a troika, rode to the hunt with Artinov, performed in one-act plays, dined out and saw less and less of her family. Now they ate alone. Poitr Leontitch was drinking more than ever, there was no money and the harmonium had been sold long ago to pay off a debt. The boys would not let him go out in the street by himself now and were always looking after him to see he didn't fall; and when Anna came riding by them in Old Kiev Street, drawn by a pair of galloping horses, Artinov up on the box instead of a coachman, Piotr Leontitch took off his top hat and was going to shout but Petya and Andrusha took him by the arms and pleaded:

"There's no need, Father . . . That will do, Father. . . ."